Where have all the men gone?
Find a playground, any playground,
and buried deep within its memory,
you'll find them there!

THE DEATH OF THE PLAYGROUND

How the loss of 'Free-Play' has affected the Soul of Corporate America

Kurt Philip Behm

authorHOUSE®

AuthorHouse™
1663 Liberty Drive, Suite 200
Bloomington, IN 47403
www.authorhouse.com
Phone: 1-800-839-8640

First published by AuthorHouse 6/4/2009

ISBN: 978-1-4389-3714-4 (sc)
ISBN: 978-1-4389-3715-1 (hc)

Library of Congress Control Number: 2009902328

Printed in the United States of America
Bloomington, Indiana
This book is printed on acid-free paper.

Playground: "A field or sphere of unrestricted pleasurable activity"
(The Farlex Dictionary)

The Playground of his youth would become the wellspring of his life. All decisions would be run through its filter of right and wrong.

Without his eight years at the Playground, Kurt's life would certainly have been different. Not only for him, but for the millions of other boys of his generation.

DEDICATION

To all the Playground Gremlins and Merlins hidden deep within the Woods, that an eight year old boy had to burn down to find.

May their spirits stay alive to awaken future generations now temporarily asleep, deprived of the joyous harmonies of 'free-play.'

INTRODUCTION

Where is the Soul in today's modern corporation? Is it on the assembly line, the office staff or maybe in top management? It should be found in all of those places. If the men working for those corporations were born before 1960, that Soul was almost certainly formed and developed in a Playground. Playgrounds were nestled in the union of instinct and opportunity, and wrapped in the smell of freshly cut grass. They gave to us our first and most important lessons in life. For those of us lucky enough to grow up on one, all of life's great principles and lessons seemed buried somewhere between first and second base.

Those messages were formal while being formless, and they had a magnetic quality to unify rather than divide. They were sacred and we passed them on! And this all happened without our knowing it!

Each Playground had its own Legends and its own History, but all of them were related by the effect they had on the character and souls of the boys who played there. From San Luis Obispo to Brooklyn Heights, those messages sang out in a virile harmony. They were timeless, and they echoed from the places where Men were made.

Our Mothers were the caretakers of our basic needs, but our Playgrounds were the custodians of our hopes, our aspirations, and most important our dreams.

We walked into the Playground as little Boys,
and exited 8 years later as Men.

I wrote this Book about the generations of Men whose childhood lessons were seamless, and for the Men raised in the last thirty years whose lessons were not. The Playground experience had a timeless quality, unbroken for many generations. The men raised there fought and won two World Wars, developed the mighty corporations, and wrote the great books of twentieth century literature. These Men knew they were Men, and they knew where it first happened. They also knew how to pass it on.

The bridge to this type of Manhood had no toll taker, and its crossing was paid for with hard fought experience. We thought these bridges were permanent and an ongoing part of our history, but they are spiritually crumbling today. If you look in almost any American neighborhood you can see them. They are the Parks, Recreation Centers, and organized Ball-fields that before 1970, were just called 'Playgrounds.' They were about much more than just play; they were about 'free-play.' The loss of 'free-play' is the greatest casualty resulting from the death of our nation's Playgrounds.

The best of memories don't fade with time, they shape it! The Playgrounds of America gave birth to these memories and then kept them alive. They sculpted and structured the lives of the fast growing Men who wandered their fields and courts. They gave meaning and purpose to their everyday lives, shaping and forging character with every daily event.

At their essence, they were the connection that bound generations of developing Boys together, as they went through the process of becoming Men. The Playground became indelible and permanent within the hearts and minds of every male who passed through its gates. The lessons it taught us changed us forever, and these changes have stood all tests of time.

It is the concept of 'free-play' that the Playground gave birth to and became its absolute master. In the absence of adult supervision, magic happened. It is this magic that is missing within the heavy structure of the Soccer Moms and T-Ball Dads of today. With the best of intentions they run highly supervised and organized programs where the opportunity to create your own games, make up your own rules, and deal with whatever comes along no longer exists. Unknowingly, and only trying to help, the parents call all the shots. In so doing they ruin the whole concept of 'free-play.'

Many of the things that parents now do for their kids, they used to do for themselves. These things, and the events that ensued were critical to their adolescent development. Every evening they would tell the stories about these events to their parents at the dinner table. Their Mothers and Fathers were almost never there to see the actual events happen, but they grew up on a playground too and therefore appreciated their meaning. These kids became the creators and historians of a universally shared adolescence. They played together in all weathers and seasons from ages eight to fifteen, and benefited from a 'free- play' experience so powerful that no other time in their lives would ever equal it.

This is my story, but I shared it with the millions of Boys of my generation. We were all connected through the Playground to the legions of boys that went before. In an attempt to recapture the 'essence' of that male adolescent experience, let's first take a look at what we've lost.

Circa 1953

My first Playground was 60" square. Inside it, I was taught my first important lessons in life. I learned I could pull my cousin Jimmy's hair, but not my cousin Tommy's. Tommy was a year older than I was and had a bad attitude. His corner of the Playpen definitely belonged to him.

Within those wooden rungs there was a power structure, a pecking order, and a sense of territoriality.

How did I learn these things? They were buried deep within the DNA of that Playpen atmosphere. The really meaningful activity that happened inside that 5' X 5' only revealed itself **when our mothers left the room**. Only then did we become the little masters of our own fates, experiencing the pure joy of 'free-play' for the first time.

Fast forward from my youth and much has changed. The great lessons of a Man's life that were first learned in the Playground, often times go unlearned today. From the Playpen to the Boardroom, successful men had always followed a well-worn path in their development. That pathway is now covered over with artificial technology, and often violent media content. Where are our Playgrounds today? If we look hard we will see that they're still there, sitting silent like a bell waiting to be rung, chiming out the joyous tones of freedom and togetherness.

As a group, the boys of my generation played and explored, we fought and we learned. We did this together, within a system that was handed down from older boy to younger boy, all without the presence of constant parental supervision. It was wrapped in the Playgrounds great gift to us all ....

The gift of 'free-play'

CHAPTER ONE: BILLY AND MAX

Emergency Board Meeting:

Proposed Cuts- 5 Branch offices, 3000 Jobs

Net Effect- Short term gains to appease the shareholders

True Cost- Permanent impact on 3000 lives for temporary gains

Sitting alone in his chair at the end of the long table, Max leaned back and closed his eyes. The last of the board members were long gone and the room was quiet and dark. His mind now drifted back as it often did to the security of his youth. He was mentally and spiritually now back in his playground.

The big county-wide basketball championships ended tomorrow and his team had made it to the final game. He received a phone call tonight from a kid who lived in another neighborhood, offering to play for Max's team in the championship game. This kid was a township all-star and would virtually assure Max's team of winning the trophy. To do this Max would have to let one of his players go.

Billy, who was the weakest player on the team, was also the one who worked the hardest. No one had given more of themselves to get the team to where they were now. To let the new kid play, Max would have to let Billy go. Did he really want the championship that much? Could he look into those eyes and then live with that feeling forever? Was he man enough to do the right thing?

Max's team lost that championship game the next day, but Billy was voted the most valuable player. He had one point, the result of being fouled and making one shot out of two when the game was out of reach. They lost the county championship that day but walked away with something much bigger as a team.

It was Billy who would finally win, and on a national level. Ten years after that county game he captained two 'Special Olympic Basketball Teams' to national championships. When they presented him with the team trophy Max was standing by his side. He was prouder in that moment of Billy than in anything he had ever accomplished on his own. Who knows what would have happened to Billy had he been dropped from that playground team so many years ago. Max said the feeling at the awards dinner that night when the moderator spoke about Billy was beyond measure.

Max and Billy remained the best of friends for thirty more years. Max would often visit Billy at his group home and had a backboard and rim installed for him behind their house. Beyond measure, is what Max saw in Billy's eyes the night he died in October of last year. Beyond measure, is the damage the board was asking him to approve just to appease the shareholders.

He opened his eyes and leaned forward in his chair. He now knew what he had to do.

Although not created there, the soul of a company can be lost or saved in its boardroom. Inside those heavily paneled walls its directors should be a beacon, guiding their companies to new wealth and prosperity. This should be their finest hour. Character should never come under question or attack. Their integrity should be above reproach. If these board members were born before 1960, there's a good chance of that being true. If they spent their youth on a public playground, there's a better chance still.

Three years later with his company intact, Max merged with his largest competitor. All current employees were now part of the new company and shareholder value was increased four fold. Making the right decision in the quiet darkness of that empty boardroom was the right thing to do. No longer vilified, Max is now considered a visionary and leader within his Industry.

Learning early to fight for those rights of entitlement.

CHAPTER TWO: THE EPIPHANY

It's mine, no it's mine. BANG!

The red truck sat in the middle of the sandbox as both boys watched and waited intently. Ultimately, Davey reached for the Truck first as Kurt then made his own move to claim it for himself. The collision happened at Mid-Box, and a mighty tug-of war then ensued. Davey and Kurt struggled to claim the most basic of male adolescent proprietary entitlements, the right to say ……………. 'that's mine!'

In a Titanic battle for control, they pulled the Truck back and forth between themselves. Davey swung first and smacked Kurt as they battled for the Truck in the sand. Kurt retaliated by grabbing Davey's hair, and now both Mother's were screaming and frantic and caught up in the middle of the Toddler's skirmish.

What was only a moment ago a very peaceful scene had denigrated to life at its most basic level. As they separated the two combatants, and wrested the Truck away from both Boys, Kurt and Davey made real eye contact for the first time.

The Fire in their eyes turned from anger to wonderment, and then to broad smiles, as they recognized each other for the first time for who they really were. They were two Men on the way to doing manly things! As their Mother's made profuse apologies to each other, the eye contact between Davey and Kurt remained unbroken.

In the confusion of the sudden conflict, both Mothers seemed to be on the verge of nervous breakdowns, but all Kurt and Davey could do was smile.

This was their genesis. This seemingly innocent test of wills, and the courage to defend it, foretold at the most basic level what would

5

happen to both boys in only five short years. In five years they would both be at the Playground, and Mom wouldn't be around.

On this day though, in our little park and all over America, it was hard to know how much greatness was really birthed in those Sandboxes.

'Anything seemed possible'

CHAPTER THREE: INITIATION AND THE URGE TO EXPLORE.

The Pull was too strong. The swings and the sandbox too timid. We had to get to that Pond.

My Mother was a Tomboy and Athlete, who grew up during the Great Depression. She was the oldest child of a working class family and she had married well. In 1952 she was living the American Dream, and I was 4 years old. She had Captained her high school basketball team, and now she and her best friend Mary were coaching basketball at a local Women's college.

She was a 'Jock'

She believed that boys should be 'rough and tumble' and in May of 1952 took me to the playground for the very first time. **My young life would never be the same**.

The small park at the end of our street had Swings and a Sandbox, but of most interest to a 4 year old was the Pond. As my Mother pushed me on the swings, and played with me in the sand, my mind and my eyes could not stay off that Pond. My Mother wasn't a great swimmer so she tried very hard to keep me away from the water, but the harder she tried, the more I wanted to break away from her safety net and explore that Pond.

In the Ponds reflection I saw my future, not in so many words or in something I could tell her at the time .... but I just knew.

I knew even then that life had to have adventure, and Mother's have a tendency to filter that out with their protective instincts. I also knew that adventure was going to be even better if it was shared, and better still if shared with my best friend Davey Hill. Our Mother's were good friends, and that friendship would spell opportunity for Davey and I.

On this day, Davey and his Mother had been building a sand castle in the far right corner of the sandbox. Davey's Mother would fill the bucket with sand, wet it, and turn it upside down to form the turrets of a castle. As soon as the new turret was set, little Davey would annihilate it with a big jump and crash landing, ending up butt first on top of the wet formed sand.

I wanted some of that. I wanted it bad, and I wanted to do it with Davey.

This was the first shared 'lesson' I learned in the playground. It was how to get out from under our Mom's security blankets, and even to be a little devilish right in front of them. It was a conscious act of breaking away and asserting our independence. But even more than that, it was a way to make Davey laugh, because now I knew the secret too.

There was now a space inside both of us that only the company of men could ever fill. That day, while crushing sand castles, we could feel a coming-of age, a time when all boys were going to be at the playground.

We couldn't wait for it to be our turn.

The rest of that afternoon our Mother's tried to lure us back to the safety of the swings and the sandbox, but for us there was only one real place to be, and that was the Pond. In the beginning, Davey and I would only marvel at our reflections, intertwined, side by side on the Ponds surface. We became one in our pursuit of independence, and there would not be one inch of that Pond that we wouldn't eventually explore.

There was an old wooden bridge over the Pond that we would hang from, dangling our feet in the water and occasionally falling in. It was cold, it was dark, and it was magic. Most of all, it was what our mothers didn't want us to do. You could hear our shared understanding of this in the tenor of our boyish laughs, as our Mothers yelled and tried to chase us off that bridge.

We just knew .... we were really onto
something !

Later in life that Pond came to represent what the more timid of
the boys in our group feared. It had no rules like a jungle gym or
a swing-set, and had its own unwritten set of challenges. After my
Parents moved to a 1960's post WW2 subdivision, the 'Pond' in our
new Playground was an old barn that was leftover from the farm that
had been there before.

It was big, it was dark, and it had many secret doors and passageways
that we loved to explore. We would push each other down its grain
chutes, jump from its hay lofts, and the bravest of us would climb up to
the cupola on the top of its roof. Several of the less daring boys would
never come inside, but for the rest of us, in the looming presence of
that old barn, our shadows grew.

Years later when starting a new job I always tried to locate the
company 'Pond'. It was always the road less traveled, or that impossible
project or account that no one could sell. I always felt the hair on the
back of my neck stand up when a seasoned company veteran explained
to me why their particular Pond could not be crossed.

At moments like that, my mind was instantly transported back to
the Playground, and my soul came alive !

The time honored tradition of successful development from adolescence to manhood

CHAPTER FOUR: THE LADDER

*Big Guys above, and little Guys below, the Ladder had
to be climbed.*

The Ladder was the backbone of every Playground. It was the
ascending series of challenges and initiations that tested all boys, ages
8 to 15. It had 8 rungs which had to be climbed and was the very
structure the Playground was built on. You might have been short, or
even worse slow, but you still had to try.

Trying, and its ugly stepchild failure, measured you as you climbed
the Ladder. Trying your best always pointed you in the direction
upward, where older and more advanced boys had gone before. Their
helping hands were always there to pull you up, or catch you if you
fell, with the occasional motivating slap as each rung of the ladder was
either made or lost.

How many of today's executives appreciate every rung of their
corporate ladder, recognizing each step as essential for them to succeed?
How many take the time to create a perpetuating environment where
the new can flourish and recognize the road-signs to success? How
many executives realize that it's the game itself, played well, fairly,
and as a group that gives a company its identity. Without a strong
corporate identity, it's hard to create an atmosphere of excellence, where
a workforce can maintain an ongoing level of success!

Too often we compete with blinders on, resulting only in self-
centered tunnel vision. To those around us, this makes us seem arbitrary,
self-aggrandizing, and concerned only with ourselves. To truly win, we
must win together, as a country, as a family, and as a corporation.

The Ladder of Success in the Playground instilled that ethic!

As a squirt, which was the entry-level position at the Playground, you may have been the last one picked, but you were in the game. You may have been called 'butterfingers' but you could learn to block. The Playground exacted its own system of value, and **trying and teamwork were at its very heart**.

How hard you were willing to try, and your acceptance by the guys win or lose, was what forged your playground identity. Trying and never giving up were absolutely necessary if you were ever going to get to that top rung. You might someday become famous as the President of I.B.M., but your Playground identity would outlive it. You carried it from the inside out. Nicknames became badges of honor that were earned by your Playground exploits. They were personal, they had special meaning, and they belonged to you and you alone. With sweat, and maybe a few broken bones you had earned them. Forever, the nicknames still linger in the air above the Playground, ready to be summoned again if the spirit fails. Go back and visit yours as I often do mine; close your eyes and remember. You will hear them too!

In the Playground, we had our own language with its own meaning. 'Slowpoke' may have been the fastest kid in the park, and 'Slim' may have been the heaviest, but it worked for us. We finished each other's sentences, told each other's jokes, and exaggerated in the extreme about our Athletic conquests. We did this until our noses were longer than our dreams, and then we laughed.

We laughed a lot !

It was a society of inclusion, where kids played all the parts. The team was the thing. We fought among ourselves, but never in front of guys from another neighborhood. How many young corporate executives could duplicate this team strength and loyalty inside their own company's today. How many even try to be a functioning part of the group, putting the greater good of all ahead of their own.

Where were their Playground's?

All of these great things happened to us in the Playground without any active parental supervision. Dad was at work and Mom was at home, but for a short time every afternoon and all day Saturday and Sunday, we were the new centurions. Our Playgrounds were governed by a time honored tradition and rite of passage. Those traditions are what made it special, respect for them is what made it work! We understood the Playground instinctively and the Playground understood us. We were accepted! We weren't just tolerated or put up with as in 'Children should be seen and not heard'. Inside its gates we had status, and we knew we were special!

It might look small and overgrown today, but in our world the Playground was large and full of promise. It was the promise that kept us coming back. We climbed its ladder and dreamed its dreams, always returning the next day to be considered 'one of the guys,' one of the Playground 'regulars.' We knew we could all be Willie Mays or Mickey Mantle if we just practiced a little harder. The Playground made us feel like we always had a shot. What could be better than that? Every kid back then could grow up to be President.

At least in his dreams.

THE 8 RUNGS OF THE LADDER:

1-<u>Walking thru the Gate</u>: Letting go of Mom's hand and making your entrance.

2- <u>Sitting and Watching</u>: You're seating place along the sideline was important and defined your status as a squirt. As you proved your mettle, you got to sit closer to the action. From here you could chase a loose ball or retrieve a football that went into the creek. These were cherished things to a squirt.

3- <u>Identifying the power structure</u>: You had to know who was at the top, middle and bottom of the Playground hierarchy. This would help you avoid costly mistakes as you climbed higher, and serve as a guidepost on your way to the top.

4- <u>Learning the rules:</u> Both the formal and sometimes more importantly the informal rules, lead to acceptance into the group. Loyalty, learning to keep secrets, and the willingness to share would go a long way toward your becoming a valued member. Learning with your mouth closed and your ears open went a long way too.

5- <u>Finding your own personal 'Big Guy' or mentor:</u> You really hoped one of the older Guys would take you under his wing. This would elevate you in status, and put you on the fast track to success.

6- <u>Evaluating your strengths</u>: How did you stack up against the other guys? This was constant, and gave you an ever-changing 'barometer' as to how you were developing as an athlete, and an all around good kid. The biggest legend to come from my Playground had the slowest start, but he never quit. You just had to stay with it.

7- <u>Creating your Playground 'Rep':</u> This took years and would glorify your place in Playground history, a history that was almost always immortalized and 'carved in the tree.'

8- <u>Leaving something behind and sharing what you learned</u>: You had to be willing to give back to the never ending new round of 'Squirts' and transfers that kept the Playground fresh and vibrant. You were now a part of the permanent record, a vital link between present and past

'*What my Playground looked like shortly after the fire*'

CHAPTER FIVE: BURNING DOWN THE WOODS

At less than ten gallons an hour, the little hose fought a futile battle against the raging fire, but the little fireman would not give up.

When I was 8 years old I burned down the woods behind my house. The entire woods! The aftermath of this fire, and I assure you it was unintentional, would eventually become our Playground.

It started one evening when my sister and I were playing Badminton in the back yard. We used to think it was great fun to hit the shuttlecock as hard as we could, and watch it travel through the pine branches overhead, coming down hopefully on the other side of the net. Regularly the 'birdie' would land in one of the tall pine branches that overhung our net, temporarily calling a halt to the game.

We thought we had a simple and safe solution for retrieving the birdie. We would take Mom's aluminum clothes pole and throw it high into the tree until it made contact, knocking the birdie loose, and causing it to fall harmlessly to the ground. What we didn't know was that three electrical power lines ran concealed through the branches, just fifteen feet above where we were playing. The pines towered high above a chain link fence that separated our housing development from the woods out back. On my third try to get the birdie to drop, the aluminum clothes-pole made contact with the three electrical wires. I actually threaded the three wires with the aluminum pole and that's when the excitement really started. Don't ask me how the pole was able to intertwine itself within the three wires. I'm sure I couldn't do it again in a million years, but as we found out later that night, there were greater forces at work.

The three lines exploded in a fury of fire and sparks. It looked just like the finale our high school put on every Fourth of July. There were explosions of light everywhere. My Dad said it reminded him of when he was in Guadalcanal. Unsure of what to do, I ran to the outside water spigot and got my Mother's small garden hose to try and fight the fire. This scene was so comical to the firemen when they arrived that they took my picture 'fighting' the fire. This picture ended up in our local neighborhood newspaper and afforded me no little dose of notoriety. Not only did I start the fire, I was also the one trying to bring it under control. I felt terribly responsible, even though it was an accident. The township and the Fire Department wrote this one off to 'boys just being boys'. The beautiful woods behind our house was now ashen and black, and on rainy days it smelled really bad.

I had burned down the woods, and I mean all of it.

This is the story of how our Playground began. The following spring the owners of the now fire ravaged estate transferred the tract of land to our township. The township board had a community meeting and it was decided that the best use that the land could be put to was recreation. Recreation in 1958 meant a Playground.

I have always credited myself as being the visionary founder of our sacred spot. Being a real visionary of course would have meant that I set the fire on purpose, and that just wasn't so. That day I was just the 'instrument' of a higher power.

In business we often need a fresh start, and we always need to know the consequences of our actions. This results from doing our homework and due diligence, and looking at all possibilities. I obviously hadn't done mine or I would have known about the electrical wires in the trees. On that day I was very fortunate, as the township fathers had the foresight and vision to see something wonderful, now buried deep in the embers of the woods.

Blessings and opportunities often come out of left field and from the ashes of misfortune. We have to learn not only to think outside the box, but to embrace and reward this kind of thinking. Making lemonade from lemons is what happened when our township made a Playground out of my mistake. It just took the right people to see it. They turned what started out as a bad situation, into a new beginning for all the boys in my neighborhood. The right people + opportunity = magic!

Our neighborhood, and all the Boys who lived there, would never be the same!

Sometimes access is everything

CHAPTER SIX: THE HOLE IN THE FENCE

Five seconds through, and five seconds back. That's all it took for what used to be a ten minute walk.

A chain link fence separated my backyard from the Playground. It was almost ten feet high with three strands of barbed wire across the top. To an eight-year old boy this barrier not only prevented my entry, but came with an added cruelty. I could see through the fence to where the other kids were playing, but I couldn't get in without walking a block and a half to the east gate of the Playground. This was at the end of a path wedged between two houses where two of my mothers best friends lived. This made sneaking into the Playground when I was supposed to be doing homework or watching my sister next to impossible. From my room I could see and hear the other guys 'climbing the ladder' without me. I was determined to get in, but more than that, I had to get in. I wanted and needed what was inside.

Every Christmas, my Grandfather would drop off a live Douglas Fir tree in a galvanized tub that we would take inside and decorate for the holidays. After the New Year we would then plant the tree in the back yard. My Father always planted these in front of the fence and underneath the tall pines that separated our back yard from the park. He did it to hide the fence, but to me what he was really hiding was my view of the Playground. I was now slowly loosing the ability to see into the place that I so desperately loved, as well as being physically kept out. The Fir trees, each one about a foot taller than the next, denied me any visual feedback as to what the other guys were doing inside.

It was behind these trees that I made my first corporate decision. Corporate in the sense that the 'Company' I wanted, was playing Basketball not fifty feet away on the other side. With shears in hand

and shielded from view by the two biggest Fir trees, I cut a two-foot by two-foot hole in that fence. I cut the opening in the shape of the letter C. This allowed one side of the opening to remain attached, and I could then swing the twenty-four inch cutout back and forth to easily pass through. I could also hide the cutout after leaving or returning by pushing the flap back and into the fence. I had now created my own entrance into a magic world. I had severed the umbilical cord restricting my young development. The incision I made now held my personal intravenous tube, feeding who I was to eventually become.

Many times in my ensuing business career I have found access, especially easy access very difficult to attain. The memory of my fence has stood as a great reminder that there are many entrances and approaches to a situation. The front door or main gate is just one option. When what you really want lies on the other side of that fence, which could take the form of corporate gridlock, budget constraints, or bad management, you have to find that hole or window of opportunity to get through.

It's always there!

Sometimes it's just hiding behind something else like my pass through was. Even when the Playground was locked at night or early in the morning, I had a way in. Having a way in, an open line of communication, or access to critical intelligence has been pivotal in the careers of most successful executives. Access to the executive suite, the president's office or the boardroom, requires your own personal 'hole in the fence,' at some point along the way.

The great Chinese philosopher Sun Tsu talked about using 'smoke screens' as a diversionary tactic to get what you want. Under the cover of smoke you can sometimes accomplish what would be much more difficult out in the open. My Fir trees worked just fine for me. Once the other guys discovered what I had done they all started looking for their own direct access to the park. Some cut the barbed wire at the top and would climb over. This required a major effort, and was very hazardous to their Jeans or Khaki's. Some even dug a trench below the fence and would burrow under. This was also very messy on wet days. One fellow even got his parents to have a real gate cut into the fence. The only problem here was that the gate also had a lock, and yes, as you've probably already guessed, his Parents had the key. Parents, and their very involvement with our access, were a constant challenge to our determination and ingenuity.

There was one other form of access though, that was even sweeter than any of the above, and that was borrowed access. Boys that lived in houses that didn't border the Playground would borrow the secret entrances of those that did. In a corporation someone else's access is sometimes even more favorable and more direct than your own.

It was always first and foremost about getting in. We knew Mom's Station Wagon wouldn't fit through that hole in the fence. Once we made it inside, we were on our own. No way were the Mother's of the 1950's going to 'walk' into a Playground. It just wasn't their style. When they needed us, they just rang the big bell that hung outside everyone's back door. Once inside we were free to climb the Playground's 'Ladder of Success', bonded together by the adrenalin which screamed through our young veins. We were Knights Errant on a crusade of 'free-play.'

And the Playground was our Queen!

CHAPTER SEVEN: JUST IN CASE, MOM AND DAD WERE ALWAYS THERE

The Bone stuck out through Jacky's skin as my Mom quickly started the station wagons motor. The fall from the hay-loft had been too high.

Your Parents didn't accompany you to the Playground like the Soccer Moms, Hockey Dad's, and Little League Parents of today. That doesn't mean they weren't involved; they just weren't over involved. Life had more balance, and Parents didn't need to go to such extremes. How many kids today take gymnastics, piano, play a team sport or three, have a private tutor, sing in the choir, and still have trouble making simple decisions on their own?

Why should they decide when there's Mom or Dad, or both, over by the fence 'just in case'. 'Just in case' means that the parents are the kings and queens on this chessboard and the kid's are the pawns. We all know what happens to pawns. In most cases they are expendable and never grow to have much power. We used to be a nation that created legends and heroes, one where every kid believed he could grow up to be President. We really did believe that, or at least we believed we could do the next best thing and manage Nick's Toy and Hobby Shop. Managing Nick's may have been better than being president, if you poll most of the guys I grew up with.

Parents in the Playground era of my youth were like the Federal Government. They were the ultimate Bosses, but as kid's we had states rights. They were there to step in if we had a problem, but other than that we were supposed to try and rule ourselves. We were functioning autonomously under a bigger protectorate. After all, that's how they did it, and all under a dark cloud that their generation called 'The Great Depression.'

We learned on the Playground that the right decision wasn't always by consensus. Usually the only consensus, and it was invariably right, was to follow the lead of the most experienced and talented boy. We depended on him to make the right decision, and he depended on us to follow and support him. I know it sounds simplistic, but many of today's best corporate strategies become nothing more than watered down versions of an over-thought group idea when the main goal is consensus. Imagine trying to raise a family or fight a war, if all decisions had to be made that way. Someone with the skill and the training needs to decide. Then, we all need to do our part in supporting that decision. On the Playground, almost everyone got a turn at deciding, but only after they had put their time in, paid their dues, and earned the right to make decisions for others. Corporations could take a lesson from what we learned there.

Great strategies take vision, insight, and the courage to make them happen. The courage to do what you thought was right, and then stand up for it was learned first on the Playground. The reason so many startup companies grow astronomically, while many of today's corporate giants are floundering, is because in those smaller companies there isn't a committee and subcommittee riding roughshod over all the creative thinking. There's no focus group in most of these small fast growing companies, telling the visionary entrepreneur that he's wrong in one long string of endless meetings. Parents today are also frustrated and confused. They want to control and decide their child's every move, while expecting them to grow independent and strong at the same time.

You just can't have it both ways.

There's nothing wrong with diligent research, taking good advice, doing your homework, or paying attention to sound business principles, but we need to keep the horse in front of the cart. Too many great ideas get 'managed away' before they can even begin to take form. There has to be an environment of freedom for these ideas to develop and grow; an environment of inclusion where the whole really is greater than the sum of its parts. We need a corporate culture that both rewards risk taking, and provides the training to ensure its success.

The ideas that come out of these corporations also need Champions to keep them on track. Champions, like the ones that for generations were born, developed, and nurtured in the 'free-play' atmosphere of our nations public Playground's.

Your Playground probably is different today'

CHAPTER EIGHT: WHATEVER YOUR PLAYGROUND WAS

The maple branch was now a crows nest on a pirates ship. The great wooded sea battle had begun. From tree to tree we fired our mock cannons, sinking and swimming in great imagination.

Whether your Playground was three concrete steps in South Philadelphia where you played half-ball, a frozen pond in Fargo North Dakota where you played hockey, a closed marina in Marathon Florida where you pretended to be a pirate, or a baseball diamond anywhere in America. They were all connected and we were all the better for it.

Our Playgrounds were not always literal; sometimes they were figurative and totally of our own making. Put kids in almost any environment and leave them to themselves; magic and wonderment usually starts to happen. I'm convinced that as kid's we all have a gene that is only triggered when our **Parents leave the room**. It's the 'individual' inside of us coming out, and like a plant or a flower, or anything that grows, it needs its own special TIME and SPACE for that to happen.

Sometimes a Playground only exists in the imagination. This is sadly too real for so many inner- city kids sitting on the front steps of tenements, and making up stories about what life must be like beyond the ghetto. This Playground is no less real than the 10 million dollar hockey rink in suburban Toronto. In fact, in some ways it's more real. Sadly, too many of their heroes are sports and entertainment figures, who once they make it out of the inner city, rarely, if ever, come back.

The role of imagination and visualization were Playground specialties. We all imagined ourselves to be the next Willie Mays or Paul Hornung, or maybe even Spiderman. What, Spiderman is fictitious you say? Not to a group of ten-year old boys whose Fathers all single-handedly won World War II. We had no trouble seeing ourselves as the masters of our universe, just like our comic book heroes, as long as we were back home by 5:30 for dinner, because well, you know Mom.

Our Fathers read them too!

In our magical world of imagination, comic books were to be treasured and saved. We read each one at least a thousand times. They represented the world of possibility, the world of dreams, and they only cost ten cents. Superman, Spiderman, Batman, and the Green Hornet lived in our bedrooms with us at night, and we vicariously took their strengths to the Playground with us every day. Their comic book exploits were our corporate manuals and mission statements. We lived out what they symbolized every day, engrossed in the magic of 'free-play'. Our Parents (especially our Fathers) read them too. Sometimes in secret, but they did read them!

How many Parents really understand where their kids are mentally and spiritually today? Their bodies sure. They can usually tell you where their kids are physically at all times, but their hearts and minds, and their dreams? Often those things get farmed out to the supposed 'experts.' In our culture and language, the words surrogate and parent need to become mutually exclusive!

CHAPTER NINE: 'THE APPRENTICESHIP'

*Maybe if I watch his bike, or tell him his dog is really
smart, maybe then he'll pick me today.*

Fetching and chasing balls for the bigger guys was the first stage in your apprenticeship.

You would back up home plate, stand beyond the end zone, or sit behind the backboard to run after and retrieve loose balls. You felt honored and special when you brought one back and a bigger and older guys said 'thanks kid.' You learned how to mentally play the game before actually getting in. It was kind of like 'paper trading' stocks for beginning investors today.

You got to strategize with other 'squirts,' about what you would or wouldn't have done if you had been in the game. Even though it wasn't you hitting the home run or sinking the basket, you were part of the game. You were visualizing in your mind your future actions, until you were big enough to actually play.

You cheered the guys on for their great plays, you bided your time, and you learned. You learned by watching those older and better than you were. You also learned by listening to their stories and hearing how they had put their time in and paid their dues. They appreciated your cheering for them even if they didn't say it. You could tell by the look in their eyes, and in the head nod you would get back when you yelled .... *"great shot!"*

The older guys spoke with reverence about the guys that had gone before them, and the miracles those past legends had performed athletically. You longed for a time when you could meet one of these legends and maybe one of them would actually know your name. It was a caste system based on age and ability. If you played by the rules and kept your mouth shut (especially as a young guy), your time would come. You learned patience and the true value of being part of something special, something that was much bigger than you individually.

And something that worked!

You lived for those days when, for whatever reason, several of the older guys couldn't show up to play. This was usually due to Boy Scout meetings, lawn cutting chores, paper routes, or the occasional grounding. At times like this, the older guys had to let you play based on simple supply and demand. There just weren't enough older to guys to play. Now it was finally your chance to test your stuff against the accepted power base. It was at times like this that the potential was all to the upside. The big guys didn't expect you to do much, and if you did, they were your biggest fans. This was raw opportunity at its finest. You had mentally prepared yourself for this moment for so long. You were now going to get your chance.

If you did something special and unexpected in a game and showed promise, usually one of the big guys would take you under his wing. He might even try to take credit for your exploit by saying "I showed him that move," or "I taught him everything he knows." Maybe he did. This made you proud and not the least bit jealous. That big guy was accepting you into his world and validating your efforts. He might even refer to you as his 'little brother' or 'super-squirt.' In that moment the feeling of membership and entitlement was never stronger. You learned that there was value to be had at every rung of the ladder, not just the very top. The ladder is only as strong as its weakest rung at the bottom. We learned this early at the Playground, and we learned it well.

Whatever you had done, whether sinking that shot, hitting a single, or catching a short pass, it was now part of the permanent record; the Playground record. It would become an enduring footnote in your Playground legacy. These footnotes fortified your strength, allowing you to climb higher and higher.

It was a system based on trust, both in the guys that had gone before, and in the lessons and memories they had left behind. It also commanded your respect for these fellows that had gone through the system and paid their dues. They were always willing to pass on what they knew if your attitude was right and proper respect was shown. It was the willingness to 'put in your time' while waiting for your opportunity to come, that determined your success.

No shortcuts or excuses allowed!

It's a shame that in many businesses the preferred way to the top is the quick and dirty route. How many critical lessons get missed because our mouths are open when we should be listening? How many young corporate hotshots are guilty of quickly dismissing something they don't understand, something they never took the time to learn?

How many young managers fake it most of the time because they don't really trust the people they work for enough to ask for help? They expect a lack of trust from those working for them because they never learned to trust in someone or something bigger than themselves. How many division heads were never 'squirts' and ran after a foul ball, or chased a wet football into the creek? How many rely solely on sterile endowments, such as an MBA or Law Degree?

There were no formal degrees in the Playground. We didn't need them.

Everyone was recognized by the strength of their effort and their subsequent achievements. Bonuses were paid in the stories we would tell. Sit with an old Man on a porch or park bench and ask him about his life. His memory will take you back to a time when life was much more simple and pure; a time when things seemed to make sense. He will take you back to a time when his character and personality were being formed. These stories are usually best told from grandfather to grandson. Fathers are usually too busy playing by a different set of rules. It's a shame really that the magical connection between the Playground and the rocking chair has to circumvent the middle of life .... *the part we call reality.*

Inseparable for sure, and our Dogs were the only friends we had that Mom would let sleep over every night

CHAPTER TEN: FOLLOWING RULES

Hey, that's really what I meant to say.
You just heard me wrong

It's true that no society can operate without its rules and laws that allow it to function on a daily basis. These same rules however, can sometimes shut off the parts of our brains that allow us to become the best examples of ourselves. To us, the chain link fence surrounding the east end of the Playground, with the sign that said 'keep out/no trespassing' was open to interpretation at worst, and an open invitation at best.

We needed that ball!

There were 'those days', when our only baseball was one that had been covered up several times with electrical tape, and it would go over the fence and into the new construction housing site. Someone had to go get it. It wasn't that we didn't respect the construction company's right to keep us out; we just needed that ball. We were in and out quickly, respectful of their equipment, wanting only to continue our game. We were sure that if we got caught, they would understand that they now had something that belonged to us, and that gave us a one-time pass.

Many times 'rules' are created to mask limitations. If Columbus had believed that the world was flat, or Roger Banister that no man could ever run a sub-four minute mile, their great accomplishments would never have happened. The freewheeling nature of Playground games, often made up on the spot, had rules open to interpretation. This inspired in all of us what was truly possible, and taught us how to think creatively. The euphoric feeling we got from this could only be felt if you were there, and being there together always meant that life could become bigger than your dreams!

This in no way should imply that we didn't respect rules, and those who made them. We did! We truly understood them, and knew how far they could be stretched. We also knew and accepted the punishment if we pushed too far. Pushing the envelope and stretching the rules were Playground specialties .... so was accountability and responsibility.

Ramsey Clark, the Attorney General under L.B.J. said one of America's great freedoms is the freedom to protest, and if necessary in so doing, to break the law. He also emphasized you had a civic duty and responsibility to pay whatever penalty or sanction was attached to breaking that law. It was never the Playground's intent to break any laws, just to find out how much elasticity there was in the one's we played under.

This pushing ourselves against the accepted standard, and always reaching for more, created a feeling of freedom that infused itself into all of our Playground games. A game of horse often turned into a game of horse m a n u r e depending on who was making the rules. To avoid losing, an older kid could stretch the game out with more letters to help him win. He still had to make all the shots, but now he had a little more time to do it. This is like a customer extending normal payment terms based on their greater 'buying power.'

In the Playground you could break the rules and often get rewarded for it, but you always had to respect the big picture. The Playground cut you a lot of slack, right up until the time it reeled you back in with a vengeance. You could stretch the rules just so far .... and then they snapped.

It was in many ways, the most benevolent of Dictators.

You could climb the chain link fence with the ragged barbed wire top every day instead of going to the corner and using the gate. You could also use the 'hole in the fence' in my backyard if it was closer to where you lived. Every time you climbed over that jagged eight-foot fence you knew the risk, but if you were late for a game or a card flipping tourney, you judged the risk worth it. Every once in a while a kid would show up with bloody hands or torn pants from slipping as he went over the top and getting caught on its jagged points. Risk/Reward was something we learned at its most basic level.

And we learned it well!

Unfortunately today, many people are afraid to step outside the box and try something new or maybe a little left of center, something that just might make the world a whole lot better. Charles Lindbergh and Edmund Hillary knew the risks and challenges, but felt they were worth taking. Early on, we learned to assess risk based on its potential reward, and we didn't cry or whine if it didn't work out. That just wasn't the Playground's way.

The criticism for whining would be too much and too hard to bear. We developed thicker skin than that. Too often today we only look for answers inside books, computers, data-bases and corporate manuals, when many of the right answers should already be there inside us. These answers should be cloaked in the conviction of 'having been there.' Conviction, and yes, the courage to stand by it, coming from experience and knowing you're right. The 'free-play' environment of the Playground gave us that, and so much more.

Hemmingway, Schweitzer, Einstein or Melville, almost any genius that you can name, put a spin on the ball that hadn't been there before. That spin in the twentieth century was a Playground specialty.

Rules were respected and constantly amended. Usually for the better.

CHAPTER ELEVEN: NON-SECTARIAN, AND THE TIES THAT BIND

I'll trade you two Mickey Mantles for your Willie Mays and Hank Aaron.

Our Playground was made up of a diverse group of multi-racial, and multi- national kid's that were bound together by the glue that the Playground provided. You left your differences outside the gate. Inside the Playground we were all the same. Sounds simplistic I know, but we really were!

The Playgrounds glue was waterproof, usually idiot proof, but maybe most important, prejudice proof. It stuck us all to each other, and then to ourselves. Coming together as a group in spite of any surface differences, changed fundamentally who you were by yourself. It opened you up to a world of possibility. The chance to be something greater together than you could ever be alone.

It was a world that rewarded what could be done, instead of what could not. We learned that the prejudice and biases still felt by some of the older members of our families existed only within themselves. They kept them alive to feed a fear deep inside them, a fear that was passed down through many generations. It was the fear of discovering and then truly admitting, as we already knew in the Playground, that we were all fundamentally the same.

That fear never made it through the Playground's gate!

We didn't share their feelings. Just in the act of sharing and playing together, that kind of negativity never developed. The only differences we saw were real, and those differences we did see. You might have been slow, and I was fast. Maybe your sister was a pathological tattletale, or your bike was always dirty, and maybe even your dog didn't smell so good. These were real differences though, and all that other surface stuff was to our way of thinking just B. S. wrong, and a real waste of time.

The most different among us seemed to be the one's most drawn together, proof of the old adage that 'opposites attract.' The tallest guys always seemed to have the shortest sidekicks, like Johhny Mack who stood 6'2" in the eighth grade. Mack's best friend and shadow was Jimmy McGarrity who we all called 'Rat.' Rat couldn't have been more than 5' 1" and Mack could literally rest his elbow on top of Rat's head, which he would try from time to time. The downside for Mack was when Rat retaliated for this mild 'putdown', his punches being right in line with Mack's most sensitive and vulnerable areas, if you know what I mean.

The wealthier kids and poorer one's seemed to link up too. It was almost as though they instinctively knew that they could learn important things from each other. These relationships, I'm proud to report have lasted and endured until the present day. It makes my heart swell to pass one of our favorite local restaurants on a Friday night and see through the window Jimmy Cantler, the president of our local bank having dinner with his best friend John O'Sullivan. Johnny O' provides lawn care services to make his living. He doesn't own the business, he cuts the grass! They get together at least once a week, and although divided economically, and living in very different neighborhoods, their friendship remains as strong as ever. Their families are also very close. Jimmy and John have been Godfathers to each other's children and often vacation together each year when school lets out.

We all took away from the Playground what time and title could not rob us of. What happened inside that gate happened to us together and as a group. Each member of the group had value, and it was because of our differences that we were truly able to mesh. Like positive and negative charges drawn together, we celebrated our differences with humor, polite curiosity, and an underlying air of respect. It also taught us the difference between what was real and what was not.

We learned at an early age what it really meant to be a friend, and we learned above all else that our kind of friendship was REAL! This reality transcended any petty differences of race, religion, or national origin. In many ways we were the finest example of 'America's Melting Pot.' The Playground was a constant confirmation of what is too often only 'lip service' by society at large!

We truly were a community of one!

CHAPTER TWELVE: THE 'OUR GANG' PHENOMENON

Mum's the word guys, or we're really gonna pay for this one.

They were multi-racial and multi-age grouped. They were Depression-era poor, and not so poor kids playing together. They were unaware of anything or any differences other than themselves as a group, and they were in a constant state of euphoric creative activity. This best describes the 'Our Gang' Kids. It was a very popular short film series made in the 1930's and aired on television well into the 1950's. The show portrayed everyday kids doing everyday things with a joy that jumped right off the screen. They made a Playground out of everything and everywhere they happened to be, and they were always TOGETHER. They drew you into their world, and you felt like one of them.

The important word is together!

Lessons were learned, and problems were solved, <u>together</u>. Their camaraderie, chemistry and energy, combined with an overriding concern for the group as a whole, made their experiences special. The 'Our Gang' Kids, along with later examples such as 'Fat Albert and the Cosby Kids', made seemingly simple situations in a 'free-play' environment something much more than just simple.

Even though we grew up in the relative calm and prosperity of the Eisenhower 1950's, there was the recent memory of two World Wars, and a 'Depression' that we got so tired of hearing about. These events were deeply ingrained in our Parents, who loved to retell stories of sleeping three to a bed, and walking five miles to school every day, and yes, walking home for lunch too. We knew instinctively that they had been through some tough times. We also knew that they had survived it, and in most cases triumphed. This made them the perfect role models for kids looking for the 'right stuff.'

We watched our Parents all get together in the evenings during the spring and summer and basically celebrate life. They were of German, Italian, Irish, and African-American descent, all sharing their stories and celebrating their new lives. Their pasts, and religious and ethnic origins were in many cases different, but their hopes for the future were the same. This shared hope for a unified future seems enigmatic today, at best.

Their generation had won the last great war, survived an economic holocaust, and returned the country to prosperity. They did this with a sense of togetherness that I think is now lost. We talk about it, but that's not the same thing. It's very hard to have peace and understanding without shared values and experiences. We learned this on the Playground and we learned it early. We looked for common ground, not excuses to divide and separate. We celebrated our surface differences, while realizing that beneath the skin, we were all the same.

Gang is mostly a negative term in our culture today. The only characteristic the 'Our Gang' kids, shared with the destructive and malevolent Gangs of today, was the over-riding need to be together.

Somewhere deep in our natures we all want to be accepted and part of something bigger than ourselves. Unfortunately today, this doesn't always happen in a positive and constructive way. In the Playground, our inspiration and direction came from strong Parents, who were the primary and positive influences in our lives. The Gang's of today take their cues from the hopelessness and despair of what's missing in their lives, which often is a strong family unit and older people who care. They share and identify mostly with what they haven't got, instead of what they have. Their fantasy world is one not of Walt Disney or Athletic exploit, but of violence and despair, created by poverty and the drug sub-culture.

We also never heard the word 'narcissistic' in the Playground, and we wouldn't have liked it if we had. There's too much of the 'ME' mentality in the world today, and as we hear all too often, there's no 'I' in Team. The Playground was about coming together as a group in a positive way. When you were there, you knew you were part of something special, and something that lasts.

And you were always the better for it!

CHAPTER THIRTEEN: EYE CONTACT, THE 'INDIAN SIGN' AND THE ULTIMATE STARE DOWN

He can't be lookin at me, oh my God he's lookin at me!

Eye Contact wasn't always just a challenge to someone's authority or emerging Manhood. It was an implied non-verbal connection where two people had a bond.

Long before Robert DeNiro uttered those immortal words in *Taxi Driver*, "are you lookin at me, are you lookin at me?" In the Playground we already knew what that meant. Eye contact in all its various forms was the Playgrounds telegraph. It was a signal as to what was, or what was not, going to happen. To navigate your way out of trouble, you had to be able to read the signs.

An older kid may have looked at you one way if you said something stupid, but an entirely different way if you challenged his authority or tried to embarrass him and make him look bad. It was the look you got then that we all half affectionately called 'the Indian Sign.' None of us ever knew where the saying came from, but boy did we know what it meant. If a kid bigger and older than you gave you the Indian Sign, it was time to head for the hills. In the Playground, that meant either the front gate or the Woods at the back of the park, depending on which was closer. Heading for the woods was riskier, because if the older kid caught you back there, no escape was possible.

The Indian Sign was more than a look. It was a warning about what was coming, and what was coming after one of those looks was never good. When someone was looking at you with the Indian Sign, it always seemed like they were staring right through you. This was a

47

definite signal that trouble was on the way. As menacing as it was, it was far from the only kind of eye contact we had in the Playground. You could usually judge the veracity of another kid's statement just by looking into his eyes. Sometimes he would laugh or stammer, or his eyes would roll and flutter, but with careful study of the kid in question something usually gave him away. Long before the study of 'Body Language' became a hot topic, we already understood the principle behind it, and reacted to it every day. This type of non-verbal communication was truly mastered and perfected by the Playground's toughest guys.

The really tough kid's in the Playground hardly ever talked at all, they just LOOKED!

They had earned that '*look*' after many battles and Playground conquests. It was a substitute for them ever having to explain themselves. Explaining was for the lesser kid's. You never, and I mean never, wanted to get the Indian Sign from one of these Guys. Running away was probably fruitless. He was undoubtedly faster than you, and when he caught you the punishment would be even more severe. We learned early on to see the signs of trouble and anger in the eyes of our 'superiors.' It was a knowledge that saved many of us a bloody nose or black eye. Ninety-five percent of the time they were our mentors and protectors, but it was that other five percent of the time when they became the Playground's disciplinarians. They defended their honor above all else and would not be made fools of in front of the other guys.

How many of us in business afford our bosses the same air of respect?

The lesson here was that most things come at a cost and there is usually a line that should not or must not be crossed. When you do, there is a price to be paid. I'm sure the older guys didn't like dishing out our medicine anymore than we liked receiving it, but rules were rules. More than that, a guy's reputation (his Rep) was sacred. Sullying it came at great peril to your life and limb. The few and rare epic battles between two Playground Legends usually started with the ultimate stare-down. The two combatants, knowing each other so well, would search for any weakness or reluctance to 'go' in the other kid's eyes. Sometimes these stare-downs resulted in fisticuffs and sometimes not. It almost always hinged on what the one kid saw in the other kids eyes.

There were many other forms of Playground eye contact too, like the 'laughing eyes' of the kid who had just successfully told his first 'off color' joke, or the kid whose eyes were welling up with tears because he had just been hit in the head with a baseball and was trying desperately not to cry. There was also the wise compassionate look of an older kid, consoling you after you just struck out for the third time, causing your side to lose the big game. His words "nice try kid," and a friendly slap on the back, with his eyes telling you it was really alright, on that day meant everything.

Eye contact was the unspoken language of the Playground. It was honest, it was direct and it was real. In business it's often used in a game of 'spin' to see who can convince or outfox who, based on someone's individual personal agenda. It's like the poker player, who sometimes bluffs and sometimes doesn't, but is rarely honest about his intentions. The real difference is what's behind the stare. In the Playground we learned to back up our intentions and pay the consequence. Too many times in the business world these facial gestures hide shallow posturing at best.

Today, most eye contact is likely to be avoided. It is seen as an invasion of privacy or a challenge to someone's personal space. Eye contact is uncomfortable because of the weak foundations most people are now built on, and the eyes always seem to be the first to give this away. In the Playground you might get a friendly glance, an angry stare, or God forbid the Indian Sign, but you never, ever, EVER, looked away!

CHAPTER FOURTEEN: GOOD GUYS

That's all right man, never doubted you for a minute.

'Good Guys' weren't created in the Boardroom; smart guys, shrewd guys, even brilliant guys maybe, but not 'Good Guys.' 'Good Guys' were created on the Playground. The qualities of being loyal, down to earth, approachable and cheerful, with your humanity intact, can almost always be traced back to some sort of Playground. It was like sandpaper to bad qualities. You didn't last long if they didn't come off, but they usually did.

Back when we were all equal, when we weren't CEO's or Manual Laborers, when there were no Chief Surgeons, Orderlies or Firemen, we were all taking part in one of life's great journeys. It was the ritual journey from boyhood to manhood and we took this journey together because that was how it should be. This shared experience was done in the company of friends, and these friends were almost all 'Good Guys!' Coming from the Playground, what else could they be?

Today, we often rely solely on our pedigree, intelligence, education, or our training to define our humanity, but our humanity can't be defined that way. It has to be inseparable from who we are. When it is, the human spirit learns to soar and real character is formed. This was and still should be the main function of our nations Playground's, to be a place where the person always has more value than the time or circumstance.

There is a great line from the 1970 movie 'Getting Straight.' The lead character played by Elliot Gould says, **"It's not what you do that counts, it's who your are."** The Playground knew that and was the great repository of your emerging identity. It could be a stern taskmaster, but there was no better or more loyal friend. It was the place where you could be you, and only you. Not what Mother or Dad thought you should be, or great Aunt Betty, or even Father Ryan, but just you.

The Playground accepted you unconditionally, with no strings. It demanded only the best from you, the real you, and who you would become. It was also willing to wait, investing its time and wisdom in you, as vital and necessary components to the creation of another 'Good Guy.'

It had the time.

CHAPTER FIFTEEN: MY FATHER WAS A MARINE

Standing next to him at Sunday Mass was the proudest moment of my week.

My Father was a Marine (Forced Recon) and a Veteran of World War II. He was called back to be a Drill Instructor during the Korean War, and was then married with two kids and working for Procter and Gamble. He served as a Marine for three more years, training young men to go off and fight as he had just done in the last War. He was involved in many of the major South Pacific invasions of World War II (Guadalcanal, Efati, Bougainville etc) places where the Marines suffered so many tragic losses.

He believed in the Playground and all the Boys were in awe of him. He walked, talked, and acted like a Marine. Most of all he had 'the look.' It's hard to describe, but it was the easiest thing to recognize when you were in his presence. He had stature and status, and that rubbed off on me. The other guys let me know that they admired my Dad and that made me proud. Many of the Father's in our neighborhood had fought in the last two wars and they were all heroes in our eyes. They were a constant example of manhood at the highest level, and were role models that we all wanted to emulate.

My Dad had no hair on his right leg, the result of a Japanese flame-thrower on some island named Efati in the South Pacific. His teenage Playground had been the all too real Pacific Campaign of World War II. He had enlisted two weeks before his sixteenth birthday. He forged the papers and his Mother reluctantly signed them. You needed to be sixteen before they would take you during wartime. In summer I would catch all the boys looking at my Dad's right leg when he was wearing shorts and could tell that they were proud of him too. It was something he only talked about once, but it made me very proud every time I looked at his leg.

I didn't mind sharing a little of my father with the other guys. They were my best friends, and there was plenty of him to go around. In our minds he was a great man. When he spoke, all other conversations among the boys stopped and they would hang on his every word. He reveled in our Playground stories, and his charisma fired us up to play even harder. His leadership was many times unspoken but unmistakable! We didn't always totally understand what he was saying, but we knew he was a Warrior and had been to places, and done things, that we could only dream about someday doing. Most of our Fathers were like that, ordinary men called to do extraordinary things. Most had volunteered to do it. A half-century later, I'm still incredibly proud of my Dad.

He also loved to read my comic books.

We all respected what our Fathers had done, and we too wanted to sacrifice something for a greater cause. We wanted the kind of strength we saw in my Father and many of the other Dad's. We played war games in the park at night, preparing for a time when we could go and serve just like they did. The few missing teeth and broken bones the Playground claimed from us while getting ready, were minor and gladly paid. We displayed the after effects of these passing injuries with pride. We knew we could be greater together as a group, than any of us could ever be on our own. The Playground was the glue that bound us together. We truly were a team, and like a fraternity or military unit, that bonding was for life. My Father explained to me that in the Marine Corps, it was all for one and one for all. No man was ever left behind, no matter how badly wounded. The 'Corps' had a code that lived within those Marines forever. It never died!

In later years my Dad shared with me his view on meetings. He said "Son, they should last a second less than the time it takes a grenade to get to your foxhole after the enemy has pulled the pin." They should be fast and focused, with a sense of urgency, and **always about something important**. They should not be wasted hours of fact-finding confusion that somehow always seem to replicate themselves! Most important, they should end at the proscribed time, sooner rather than later.

My Dad owned and ran a well respected national sales
and marketing firm. He knew what he was talking about.

Time is the real natural resource of American Business, and someone should be accountable and responsible for why this meeting, or any meeting, occurs. No donuts please! The Marine Corps understood this and it left an indelible impression on my Father. He had great respect for the true value of time, both yours and his! He didn't waste it, or take it for granted and neither should we. At one time the Armed Services were the next step between Playground life and your chosen career. This experience bonded generations of Men in a spirit of service, sacrifice, and national unity. These Men were unquestionably better and stronger after having served their Country. I know my Father was. He often said his time in the 'Corps' was the proudest time of his life. Until his death, he had a Marine Corps Flag off to the left side of his large desk, and an American Flag off to the right. Cutting your Mothers apron strings could happen early and it was permanent. Stepping out from under the shadow of your Father could take much longer. If he was a Marine and a Combat Hero, it could take a lifetime.

Corporations need this kind of inspirational leadership too, and they need to be able to pass it on. They shouldn't be training grounds for Donald Trump wannabes. Instead they should be places that inspire their workforce to reach both individually and COLLECTIVELY, to go beyond what they have done and accomplished before. The real teachers eventually become the students of their charges, like *the child is father to the man.*

The strong man passes his strength willingly when the right student appears. That student is usually the one initially hesitant and unwilling to accept the teacher's strength. He is usually the right choice! The Playground let go of its heroes very reluctantly, but with time and transition, and based on the right stuff, new heroes always appeared. Every CEO needs to be bringing along his second in command or heir apparent, even if they are still in development and now known only to him.

If it takes a village to raise a child, then it took the village Playground to raise that child to Manhood. We were lucky, our Playground was four acres of sylvan suburban grassland. We were safe inside its protective fencing, but we could still feel the aftermath of what had happened just ten short years before. Those Wars instilled a pride and greatness in the Men that were lucky enough to return like my Father, and they willingly shared that pride and greatness with us. That pride is very much alive and within me today!

'Semper Fi, Dad'

CHAPTER SIXTEEN: MY GRANDFATHER, MY FIRST BEST FRIEND

It was the fourth quarter of the last game of my High School career. The Assistant Coach said "your foot's broken." The words I heard next were from my best friend, "don't worry son, it'll be alright."
.... Pop was down on the field

My Grandfather, who we all called POP, was a hero and local legend beyond the Playground. He had played Baseball back in the twenties and thirties, and was an icon on all of the ball-fields and Playgrounds for miles around. He enjoyed nothing more than driving by in his big truck and beeping his horn, validating the epic struggles going on inside the fence that day.

Pop believed in the Playground, and the construction company that he and my uncles owned provided free snow plowing of the Playground's courts and parking lot through the long cold winter. He hated to see us miss even one day at 'free-play.' He never lost the sense and spirit of play inside himself. Most people who knew him well said it was the part of Pop that they loved the most.

Pop never came through the gate in the parking lot at the north end of the Playground. He had too much reverence and respect for what was going on inside to do that. He just parked his International 220 Truck in the north end lot, and watched all the boys being what he could no longer be. He used to say we were 'free and full of it.' Pop was the one who was always there. When Dad was out of town, Pop was there to take me to practice, drive me to school in bad weather, and just be there if I needed someone close. All through school he never missed one of my games, not one. He was a man's man, with a boy inside, and the first true love of my life. He has now become an even bigger part of me as I have grown older, even older now than he was back then. I would be much less today without his wise counsel. I wouldn't have the great Wife and Kid's that I have, if he had not loved me the way that he did. I just wouldn't be who I am.

He didn't teach me so much what to do, he left that for my Mom and Dad. He taught me rather how to enjoy and revel in what I did, and how to love life. He also taught me the true meaning of family and friends. Will Rogers once said he never met a man he didn't like. Well, neither did my Grandfather, and I never met anyone who didn't like him. He understood how important the Playground was to developing boys. He would sometimes make excuses to my Mother and Grandmother, getting me out of chores and back inside the fence. Pop was still playing 'club baseball' when he was well into his fifties. He was a catcher and a good one.

If his batting skills had matched his ability behind the plate, I'm sure we'd be visiting him in Cooperstown every year.

Pop worked well into his seventies and became even more valued by our entire community as the years went on. His was a very big and extended family, of which he was the beloved head. He made every grandchild feel like *THEY* were the one that really had the special relationship with him, and he had twenty one of us to look after. Talk about multi-tasking and juggling several balls in the air at the same time. He was a true master!

How many times do companies get rid of their most senior, experienced and dedicated employees, based solely on their age? How many companies lack a repository, where veteran employees with decades of experience and contributions can be tapped for their knowledge when difficult situations arise? How many companies fail to honor their own pasts, one's that these older workers helped to create. Without my Grandfather there to offer his guidance, my life would certainly have been different. Corporations are much less (and different) when they abandon their retired workers too.

I would have been much less!

How many companies simply don't care, or cavalierly dismiss what these aging warriors did for the company when it was 'their time.' We need to embrace these elder statesman as our 'Chairman's Emeritus,' knowing things that we don't know. How could we? In most cases we never even asked them and many times we should have! The Supreme Court of the United States is our greatest repository of intellectual free thought. It is populated by Justices, most of whom are beyond mandatory retirement age in today's corporate world. In many firms, these great minds would be summarily dismissed per some arbitrary corporate guideline. A testament to the wisdom of our founding fathers is that these appointments are for life, a lesson we should learn in the running of our own companies.

My Grandfather never mentally or spiritually left the Playground and he kept it open in all weather and available for us. He carried its message, long after he could no longer play the games himself. It was the true spirit of 'free-play' alive and inside of him that made him the great and special man that he was!

CHAPTER SEVENTEEN: ALLIANCES / DIVESTITURES / MERGERS & ACQUISITIONS:

I'll trade you Tommy O' and the Grinch, for Jimmy McGarrity.

As young boys we learned early about the value of the right alliances. They could win you games, and choosing correctly could maybe even win a Playground championship. Aligning yourself with the right players on the right team was one of the most highly developed Playground skills. Being with the right group of guys, all having the right chemistry and being able to play together well, usually spelled success. We learned at a young age that no one player could bring it all home. The right combination of players though, could win every time.

Sometimes you had a guy on your team that just couldn't pull his own weight. After giving him every opportunity to prove himself and get better, with no success, you were finally faced with your only viable option; dump him! This didn't mean run him out of the Playground or banish him from the group. It just meant that on this particular team, he didn't fit. Maybe you already had two short guys on your basketball team and he was short too. Three short guys on one basketball team was one short guy too many.

Maybe he was slow or couldn't dribble, or maybe he was what we called a 'gunner.' A 'gunner' was someone that shot the ball when there was no shot to be taken. The 'gunner' was similar to the corporate loose cannon who makes non-strategic moves, or goes against the decisions of the group, pressing only his own agenda. Being short or slow could usually be adapted to in time; being a 'gunner' could not. Corporate 'gunners' endanger their companies and everyone working there; their personal intentions taking precedence over what's good for the company as a whole. Their divestiture is sometimes the only solution.

In the Playground this happened every day.

Many times you could merge yourself onto another team or acquire a better player for one of yours. This normally came at a cost. For example: If eight players showed up on a given day to play basketball, and then a half hour later one more kid showed up, obviously one team is now going to have one more player than the other. A way to make this work is for the team with only four players to stay at four players, but to take the best player from the team with five in exchange for giving them their weakest player. This pits quality against quantity, and many valuable lessons get learned. If the quality players are 'on their game', their team with only four good players usually wins. If they 'slough off' or coast though they can usually be overtaken by the greater numbers represented by the five man team. It's not just about quality; it's about performance and maximizing potential too.

And many valuable lessons get learned.

How much corporate harm is done by a team that's not designed with the best chance to win?

The right move strategically can most times go either way, depending on execution. The winning team needs to have the right mix of people with the 'right stuff.' This is what wins ball games, increases share value, and helps companies to grow. Execution is best learned through experience, and the right alliance will make that experience a positive one every time.

The kind of experience we first leaned on the Playground!

CHAPTER EIGHTEEN: 'SECRETS'

I'll clean the garage til I'm 100 years old, but I'll still never tell.

Long before sayings like "What happens in Vegas, Stays in Vegas," we had a similar code. I'm sure the ad writer that came up with that slogan was a Playground kid. The Playground had its own language that only happened to sound like English. 'Yeah' could mean no, and 'right man' could mean wrong. If you were accused of being a 'good little boy' that was bad, and bordered on being called the most heinous of all things, 'a Sissy.' You would go through any initiation, take any dare, or fight any kid to avoid this handle. Being a Sissy was one Playground reality that was not a secret. It would get broadcast from the Playground tower, which in our case was the top of the chain link backstop covering home plate. Being a Sissy broke the code and everyone's honor was in question. This was our Playground and we had standards, and some things, like being a Sissy, just couldn't be tolerated.

Yes, we had our own language, our own standards, and our own signals, but most important we had and kept our own secrets. We kept them from our Parents, our Sisters, our Teachers, and sometimes from each other. A guy that couldn't be trusted to keep a secret was relegated to a different class of Playground member. He was kept on a 'need to know' basis only, and suspicion was always cast on him if something was exposed. You never wanted to be this guy. You might not be the biggest, the toughest, or the fastest kid, but you could keep a secret, and you defended to the end, the right of others to do the same.

One of the guy's Mother's was diagnosed with uterine cancer when we were in the seventh grade. It so seriously affected her son Billy that he couldn't attend school. When Mrs. Gleason got out of the hospital after a successful operation, she invited four or five of us older boys to her house one afternoon. Mrs. Gleason explained to us what had happened to her, what uterine cancer was, and what her treatment was going to be. As scary as the word cancer is today, it was ten times as frightening in 1960. The prospects for most cancer patients were not very good, and many never returned home from the hospital. This very fear had paralyzed her son Billy, and she asked us all for our help.

Mrs. Gleason asked us to reinforce in our own way what she had already told her son Billy. She told him that the doctors had fixed her problem and that she was going to get better. She also asked us to keep this among ourselves and not spread it through the neighborhood, or to any of the younger boys who might not be able to keep it to themselves. This was our secret and we felt honored and special that Mrs. Gleason had shared it with us. We also felt that in some small way we were part of her treatment. When we stopped by Billy's house or saw his Mom at the store, we sometimes winked, nodded, or touched her on the arm. We knew we were really sharing something both special and important. Mrs. Gleason died this past year after having been a cancer survivor for forty-five years. She died of what the doctors called 'natural causes' in an eighty-five year-old. Her confidence and selflessness were what inspired us to help her son, a loyal and trusted Playground friend so many years ago.

I saw Billy at the Funeral and we talked about his Mom's battle with cancer. As we talked it was as if forty-five years disappeared right before our eyes. Real friendship in times of crisis, can overcome what even the Poets and Philosophers say cannot: the ravages and effects of time.

Billy and I were brothers then, are brothers now, and we always will be. If I ever get down to my last dime, I'll use it to call Billy. I know he feels the same. The two nickels that make up that dime we earned together in the Playground of our youth.

Trust and confidence like this should play a bigger part in corporate life. Sensitive information should be valued and not used as a bargaining chip to be brokered to the highest bidder, or to boost a certain individual's career. Worse even, than not keeping a secret, is making up a secret to be used against someone to your advantage. This again, places the individual above the group, and places the whole community at risk.

One summer night we had vandals invade our Playground and knock over the fifteen foot high chain link backstop covering home-plate. The parks and recreation officials interviewed all of us to see if we knew anything. We didn't, but it wasn't long before we found out who the culprits were. The vandalism was performed by two outcast brothers, whose hobby was picking on kids much younger than they were. They also had a habit of taking things that didn't belong to them. We didn't blab this information all over the neighborhood. We knew it was too important for that, too important for the good of the Playground and we wanted the vandalism to stop.

We kept this secret among ourselves and shared it only with the township parks managers who baited the brothers back into the park to try more mischief. They did this by leaving a bag full of bats and balls overnight, underneath the now upright backstop. Two nights later the brothers reappeared, were caught, and their parents were called to the local police station. This was the most recent in a long string of offenses, and the boys were sent off to do a short stint in reform school. Our beloved Playground was once again safe and secure!

In this case it was the bigger picture, the Playground that mattered. This was hallowed ground for us, and only special people played here. The basic rules were inviolable: respect for property, the rights of the individual, and giving everyone a fair shake if they played by the rules. If we had shouted to the world what we knew about the two brothers, I'm sure they would have gotten wind of it, and never returned to the Playground to get caught and sent away. We knew how to keep important stuff like that to ourselves.

No one kid (or two) was bigger than the Playground.

We knew this lesson applied to our families, our country, and later to the companies and corporations where we would work too. That's the way our Dad's and Grandfather's felt about the places they worked. Trust and confidence was everything. If you could keep a secret and share a confidence, you were well on your way to climbing that next rung of the ladder. In fact someone would probably boost you up from behind. That's the way the Playground was. Billy Gleason and his Mom's secret, and her confidence in us to keep it, was a Playground treasure. We all shared in the pride of her total recovery that following spring.

When it rained in the Playground we all got wet. When the sun shone it was a joy that we all shared. A rising tide does indeed float all boats!

Our secrets were both kept and protected

CHAPTER NINETEEN: MALE IDENTITY AND IRON JOHN

You call me a 'girl' again and they'll find pieces of you scattered from here to the Pocono's.

I'm convinced the inspiration for Robert Bly's Pond, on which the 'Iron John' fable is based, was spiritually akin to the Playground. Whether behind a barn, in a vacant lot, or on a diamond shaped ball field, the tenets of manhood which Bly writes about are universal. They cross all cultures, nationalities, and religious boundaries; and are even more sacred than that!

The Playground defined your strengths and your weaknesses, based on a time-honored series of challenges. You may not have been the strongest kid, or the fastest, but chances are that kid was a friend of yours. You got to live that strength and speed vicariously through those better than you. These relationships formed before most prejudice, bias, or political affiliations had a chance to take root. You took pride in your own accomplishments, but what's maybe more important, you learned to boast of those of your friends.

After all, they were on your team and from your Playground, so it was almost like you did it yourself. How many corporations could benefit from this kind of camaraderie and kindred spirit? Instead of dog eat dog, we learned to rely and depend on each other's individual strengths and then leverage them. There were some guys who could take the long shot (3 pointer today), and some guys you really wanted up to bat when the bases were loaded and the game was on the line. These positions were earned by past exploits and hard work, and these guys performed with the total confidence and support of their Playground comrades. This merit-based system taught us the difference between what was real and what was phony. In those rare instances when you did get immediate gratification from the Playground, like making an unbelievable thirty-foot hook shot that no one gave you a prayer of making, the feedback from the guys spoke directly to your soul.

Most things took time, and nothing succeeds like success!

Corporations often take their staff's away to exotic places to try and bond. They do this to try and establish or reinforce a team or company identity. Obviously, they don't feel the atmosphere inside the office is always conducive to this. For us, our office (the Playground) was already an oasis of unity the moment we walked through its gates. The bond on the Playground was so strong that I still feel a strong twinge when I drive past mine today, recalling the ghosts and legends of days gone by. In the Playground you treasured the approval of your friends and they yours. You were constantly reinforcing each other's image of what you could be. It was unspoken most of the time because it was stronger than words. The image you had of yourself, as an important member of the group was always number one and that image was contained inside your emerging manhood.

There was a group identity at work, and it was all about becoming a man.

Some things were beyond question and your male identity was one of them. It was never in doubt! You might not be a homerun hitter, or the guy that could get that first down every time, but your manhood and virility were never in question. This process was insured by following the lead of the bigger and stronger older guys who you wanted to be like. They left a clear-cut path for you to follow.

The worst thing you could be called in The Playground was a 'Sissy' or 'a Girl.' You were too busy incubating your Manhood to even think about that. You loved your Mother, and maybe even tolerated your

Sister, but when you grew up you knew exactly who you were going to be like and that was your Dad! The message of the Playground may not have always been fair, but it was always consistent. It was about developing the skills that would turn you into a Man. The Playground tolerated none of the sexual confusion that exists in the world today.

The reflection in Bly's Pond, and in our creek was all
Manhood, and it was beyond refute !

Things in the Playground took time. It took years of practice, hard work, and yes, some measure of ability to become ' a Legend'. That was OK; we all had plenty of time. Today, everything moves at warp speed, from the TV kids watch to the food they eat. They want it and they want it now, and after they get it, they are seldom happy and even less often fulfilled. They are many times confused and often want to 'cry out' .... but to whom? Computers, TV's and Video Games provide little in the way of spiritual consolation. Both parents are usually at work. When they do get home, they are so spent from their hectic days that the challenges in their kid's lives become just another burden to them. Kids then turn to the only alternatives available to them, most of which are not good.

The Computer and the TV are a poor substitute for
parents

It's these two 'distraction's' that fill young minds with a combination of sensory overload, spiritual abandonment, and distrust. They create an artificial environment where kids are never sure who they really are. After watching many programs on modern TV, or playing some of the extremely violent video games available, it's no wonder a young boy can walk away feeling confused and abandoned. Who is there to explain the real from the unreal in that cyber sphere of degradation? After you've killed five thousand people in your latest version of 'Dynowar' or listened to a violent Rap Video, showcasing drugs, violence, and the objectification of women, it's no surprise that you can lose your grip on reality and the knowledge of what's right and what's wrong.

71

There was and still is a big difference.

The Playground always told the truth and protected its own. The older boys always made sure the younger ones walked the straight and narrow line, and knew what that truth was. You might not even have a Dad, but you had many 'older brothers' who knew the way. As John Fogerty of Creedence Clearwater sang in 'Down on the Corner', they were going to "try and bring you up."

It takes time and a consistent message to make a man. What TV, VCR, iPod, or Personal Computer can do that? I'm not anti-technology, I'm pro-humanity, and believe it can only be developed through the interaction of people doing humanizing things in a positive way.

Then the truest self can finally emerge.

Ask a Senior Citizen to talk about their life and so many times they will take you back to their Playground. It may have been a fishing hole, a sandlot baseball diamond, or an inner-city back alley .... but there was a place, a place where their identity was formed. I think there is a special bond that exists between Grandparents and Grandchildren that is made even stronger when these stories are shared. Grandparents have the luxury of circumspection and a greater appreciation of the true value of life. Because of the extreme pressures of their daily lives, their own children (the Parents) haven't had time for this yet. We enthusiastically appreciate wine that has aged appropriately, why not people? They are the true 'keepers of the flame' who now have the luxury of both circumspection and TIME!! They know who they are, and more often than not, they know who we are too. Their identity was never in question.

Maybe we should just ask them.

Wouldn't it be great if that proposal or report you submitted today had as much real meaning as that shot you made, or pass you caught so many years ago and made you feel about yourself today, the way you felt then. The lion inside you could then return, prowling the fields of a more modern era; your male identity stronger than ever. The meaning can still be there, it's right inside you. The Playground is what originally brought it out! There was no confusion, no mixed message, the Playground got it right the first time.

It was about being a man!

First you had to say goodbye to Mom and take that first step

CHAPTER TWENTY: THE TEN COMMANDMENTS OF THE PLAYGROUND:

ONE: SHOW UP

Hey, I told you three times to stop worrying, I'll be there.

Nothing was ever more important than being there. Rain or shine, cold weather or blistering heat, you had to show up. It was the unwritten, inviolable rule that was the backbone of Playground life.

Woody Allen said "90% of life is just showing up." My Father-in-Law worked for a large oil refinery for forty-two years and never missed a day's work. He told me there were many times during those years when he didn't feel well, and thought about not going in. He always decided against it, because that would have been letting his guys down, and that just wasn't part of his nature.

In the Playground, we understood that. How much of today's absenteeism, resulting in sub-par performance, could benefit from a real commitment to 'show up?' This is what being a 'regular' at the Playground required. You made sure to get your chores done at home, so as not to jeopardize your time inside the fence. You owed that to the other guys; they were all depending on you.

Show up!

TWO: NO WHINING

What, what was that, I can't hear you. What's that you say, I still can't hear you. Huh, huh, nope, still can't hear you .... dumb whiner!

Nothing, other than acting like a girl, was as bad as being a whiner. Whiners didn't last long in the Playground. They learned quickly, that constant complaining came at a terrible cost. The guys that got the real respect were the ones that kept their personal problems to themselves. Your Dad might be out of work or your Grandfather was sick, but you didn't dwell on it, and you certainly didn't burden others with it. More than anything, you didn't whine about it.

Eventually, everyone learned on their own what you were dealing with, and supported you in those little unforeseen ways that only good friends can understand. Sometimes this came in the form of what looked like teasing or abuse. It was really designed to get your mind off what was happening outside the park, and make you focus on what was happening now. Whiners learned to 'suck it up' or they didn't last. The whiner was the guy focused totally on himself and his personal problems. Many times with whiners these problems were more imaginary than real. You could always tell when a 'good guy' had a real problem, it was evident in the way he was trying to cover it up.

The corporate complainer is the one who always sees the glass as half empty. He is that 'bad apple' ruining the bunch, who starts everything going downhill. It's a shame more corporations don't have an executive version of our big maple tree to take the complainer behind for some positive 'attitude adjustment.' Oop's, I realize this is probably not politically correct, but then again no problem. Politics took a back seat to what was right in the Playground. Attitude was, and still is, everything.

No Whiners allowed!

THREE: NO TELLING TALES

Our lips were sealed

Long before 'Sin City' popularized "What happens in Vegas, stays in Vegas," we knew this instinctively in the Playground. You would withstand any punishment your Parents would dish out before you would tell on, or 'rat out' as we used to say, another kid. This was a matter of honor, and even though they didn't always like it, our Parents knew it too. This didn't apply to criminal acts or situations where a kid could harm himself, but other than that our lips were sealed.

You might not be the toughest kid or the best athlete, but if you were one of the guys that could be trusted to keep your mouth shut, your place in the Playground was secure.

FOUR: NO CHEATING

Hey, you stepped out
No I didn't, I was in
No, you were out when you took the shot
Well .... I tried to be in

There was 'bending the rules' and there was cheating. Believe it or not there is a difference and we learned it in detail in the Playground. Bending the rules was about interpretation and whose version was correct, but there was always a line that didn't get crossed. Crossing that line was cheating and that just wasn't allowed! Using a tree as a shield to run behind, coming out on the other side to catch a pass was bending the rules. Tripping a kid so you could catch that same pass was cheating.

Bending the rules usually involved negotiation and seasoned debating skills. This came mainly from the older guys. It helped that they were bigger too. They might tell you that your sneaker laces were undone, and when you looked down they would run by you on their way to the goal line. This only ever worked once. They wouldn't trip you, or hit you from behind on their way to the end zone, because that would have definitely been cheating.

Cheating involved a total disregard for the rules of the Playground. Bending the rules meant seeing if they had any elasticity or flexibility. In less than one season at the Playground we all knew the difference. The Playground's whole structure was sustained by its accepted rules and standards of behavior, and although we pushed as hard as we could, we all knew there was a line.

There are lines that shouldn't be crossed in corporate life too. Many cannot or will not see them. Everything to them is negotiable. We learned that something was no longer negotiable, or a matter of opinion, when someone bigger and older than us made us pay a price for pushing too far. This taught us not to stray over the accepted line. Where is the corporate leadership and vision to enact and enforce standards like this today? Where are those even principled enough to draw the lines?

Much corporate corruption it seems is actually at the top. It's impossible for the lower levels of a company to function ethically, if top management is not obeying the rules. Our Playground leaders were the best examples of what we could become, and we all tried to emulate them to the best of our ability. We tested the rules, and then we respected their borders. We didn't cheat!

Cheaters, like Whiners, didn't last very long

FIVE: NO CRYING (EVER)

Was your Mom cooking onions?

I don't want to say there was never any crying in the Playground, but you did everything you could not to. You paid the price of being labeled a 'crybaby' for weeks after the incident. Crying was mostly relegated to the younger guys. If you did see one of the older guys crying, chances are, something was terribly wrong. I remember crying only once in the Playground. It was the day I was told that one of my best friends Johnny Sanders, who hadn't been feeling well, had Leukemia. The type of Leukemia that Johnny had is one of the ones that is highly curable today. In 1958 though he didn't stand a chance. That's what I overheard my Mother tell my Grandmother one day on the phone.

The day Johnny died, the Playground not only let me cry,
it cried with me.

It's been almost fifty years and I still 'well up' when I think about Johnny and the great times we had. I never saw Johnny cry, not in the Playground, and not when he was battling his Illness at the end. Johnny's death left an empty place inside the hearts of all the Boys proud to have called him their friend. We knew our Fathers had all lost friends and loved ones in the last war, and now we had lost someone too. This, as terrible as it was, seemed to bond us even closer together. This reminder of how tenuous and uncertain life can be, made us look at each day as one to be treasured and valued.

Johnny was not one of the best Athletes or Playground legends, but he left a hole that none of the superstars or prodigies among us could ever fill. His spirit was our spirit, and he took part of us with him, while leaving us with an even bigger part of ourselves.

Johnny's memory soared above the Playground until the day I left! On my last visit back he was still there smiling, not a tear in his eye!

SIX: NO QUITTING

I have to leave, I think I hear my Mom calling.
But the games not over and you're losing 19-4.
Hey, I've got to go
.... you quitter!

Like crying, quitting was a major playground sin, and they sometimes happened together. You could be losing a game by a score of 48-0, but you didn't quit. It showed a total lack of respect for your opponent and your own team-mates. It was akin to being a traitor, and nobody wanted to be called that. Most of the kids that didn't quit developed at least a serviceable level of athletic skill, mixed with what cowboys call 'Try.' Cowboys put as great a value on the effort one gives, as the result it brings. Sometimes even greater!

Some of my fondest memories of the Playground are not of the monster grand slams, or the eighty-yard touchdown runs. They are rather of Fat Johnny trying to get around the baseline before the leaves turned on the trees, or Stu-the-Stutterer trying to explain in an excited rush that your Mom told him to tell you to get right home. He never did get that whole message out, but you learned to read his signs. Although limited athletically, these guy's never quit, and you never quit on them. You never quit on your team, your friends, or the Playground itself. Losing was the second worst thing that could happen in a game.

Quitting was the worst!

Today, when we don't get immediate results, there seems to be a tendency to abandon the project, quit and move on. If Thomas Edison, who failed so many times before succeeding, or Jackie Robinson, who had to fight opposing pitchers and the color barrier, had quit because things got tough, we would all have been deprived of two of the greatest figures of the twentieth century. The poignant movie 'Rudy' tells the story of the consummate underdog who left a lasting legacy at The University of Notre Dame because he refused to quit. His only qualification to be a Notre Dame Football Player was an indomitable spirit, and in the end that was enough. I believe he is still the only Notre Dame player to have been carried off the field on the shoulders of his teammates.

My personal favorite is Winston Churchill. His dogged determination not to quit on the British people, even when they had quit on him, reaffirms his unrivaled strength of character and conviction. He was the driving force behind defeating Nazi Germany. In so doing, he preserved freedom and democracy in a world that was teetering on the brink of disaster and totalitarianism.

His famous words ......"Never give in, Never give in, Never, Never, Never, Never give in " were his finest gift to us all. He was the towering figure of the twentieth century. No matter how tough it got, you could hear his same message carried on the winds of the Playground.

Don't quit!

SEVEN: NO BIKES IN THE BASELINE

Out of his right eye he saw his brother coming through the gate. This was gonna get ugly.

Most new bikes arrived on either Christmas day or your birthday. The ones at Christmas were no problem because baseball season was safely four months away. Birthdays were entirely different. The kid with the April thru August birthday who got a new bike, felt obligated by Playground tradition to ride it as fast and as hard as he could around and around our personally manicured baseball diamond, skidding and kicking up dirt with every turn. This usually only lasted less than two or three trips around. After that, he had to get his bike off the baseline forever. Its baptism was complete!

It was a Playground tradition with questionable origins. It was rumored to have been started by two twin brothers back before World War II who had to share one bike. They first performed this stunt at the local public school diamond because back then our Playground didn't even exist. They had to share the one bike, each riding it on alternate days. When one boy was riding the bike, the other boy was playing at the school ball-field.

One day, in violation of their agreement, one of the brothers took the bike to the diamond when it wasn't his turn. The other brother followed him there, and found the guilty brother and bicycle robber engaged in a game of 'ins and outs', with the bike lying just outside the first base line. The guilty brother was playing first base and needed to keep the bike close, in case he needed to make a quick get away.

When the guilty brother saw his angry twin coming for him, he jumped on the bike and headed across first base toward second, while yelling taunts at the now furious twin who was still afoot. Around and around the diamond, the bike-less twin chased his felonious brother, while the rest of the guys in attendance nearly died of laughter.

Finally, after at least a dozen trips around, and too tired to go on, the guilty brother crashed the bike in a heap between second and third base. The brother who was afoot, 'attacked' his twin and they wrestled in the dirt as the rest of the guys watched. Finally, both laughing, filthy, and now exhausted, they picked up the bike and moved it off the field. The telling of this story is the stuff 'Playground Legends' are made of and was required knowledge if you were one of 'the Guys.'

It sometimes sounds crazy I know, but like Philadelphia's Mummers Parade, Mardi Gras in New Orleans, and that great Spitting Contest in Oklahoma, tradition is well, tradition!

Forever, it was a rite of passage that all new bikes had to do their stint around the baseline, but after that one time they had to be GONE. On that day, I'm sure this story injected a lighthearted zaniness into what was normally an intense game, and it reminded all who were there not to take themselves too seriously. I know it always worked when we took our ceremonial trips around. This is a lesson that some high-ranking C.E.O.'s could learn. When a bike shows up in their baseline, they often explode and self-destruct, when maybe they should look a little closer.......... and lighten up!

It's not always just about the X's and O's! Sometimes we all need to poke a little fun at ourselves. Humor is sometimes the currency still tendering, when all other strategy and planning has failed.

'No Bikes allowed !'

EIGHT: NO DOGS ON
THE PLAYING FIELD

My dog didn't do it, your dog did it!

If there was one thing more coveted and revered than your bike, it was your dog. He could be a purebred or mutt, but he was yours. Through thick and thin that dog was with you, just not on the playing field. Nothing was worse than running for a groundball, only to step in some freshly deposited pile of poop, compliments of one of the Playgrounds canine regulars. Even grass stains were easier to get out than that certain smell that only your loving pooch could contribute.

Try as we might, we couldn't always keep the dogs off the field. Many of them had retriever bloodlines and couldn't help but chase the ball when it careened off some kids bat and headed toward the fence. Of course once they caught it, they thought it was great fun to play the doggy version of keep away, which always took several minutes of strenuous running on our parts to end. We never complained, or banned the dogs from the Park, we just learned to adapt.

Today, most playgrounds have a 'No Dogs Allowed' sign on them. Our dogs were as good a friend as we had in life and the only ones Mom would let sleepover every night. Everything in life doesn't always work according to plan, but you can learn to adapt to most things by staying open minded and flexible. Humor helps too! Most distractions just have to be managed and they are rarely fatal. Sometimes they even hide or conceal a hidden asset.

Let a dog run across your diamond once in a while, just be mindful of the poop!

NINE: NO BALL WAS TOO BATTERED

Who's got the tape?

New Balls were expensive and they tended to wear out quickly when you played with them on grass, asphalt, concrete, and sometimes even crushed stone. New balls were to be treasured and maybe even autographed if your Dad took you to see the Phillie's or the Orioles. They would sit on your dresser or nightstand; to be handled and played with only in your room. They were reserved for special things, like playing catch with your Father or Grandfather, or showing your little brother how to properly form that split-finger fastball.

Old balls were not a problem though. Every neighborhood kid was as gifted as a surgeon, when it came to extending the existing balls life with electrical tape. Duct tape was option two, if no electrical tape was available. Leather covers wore off the balls quickly, but they could easily be replaced by the endless supply of electrical tape that we had strategically hidden around the field. Of course the tape had been 'contributed' by one of the neighborhood Dad's, who just happened to be, and you guessed it, an electrician.

Electrical tape was the tape of choice because it conformed to the ball, could be stretched tight, and handled scuffing really well. It was practically waterproof too. With an endless supply of electrical tape a kid could keep the same ball going all season, if he didn't lose it, have someone's dog steal it, or watch it disappear into the creek. When electrical tape or duct tape wasn't available we would resort to masking tape. This was only a temporary fix because the masking tape was fragile and needed to be constantly reapplied to the ball. If you tagged one just right 'off the bat,' the masking tape would start to unravel as the ball went high in the air. This would resemble a kite with a long tail flying behind it. Of course we thought all of this was great fun, and every kid wanted to be the one to send the tape reeling.

When I think about how much joy we got from those heavily 'doctored' balls I can't help but think how disposable things seem today. Tragically, some people get treated that way too. We would no more throw that ball away than we would have kept Fat Johnny from playing in a game. We found value in almost everything we did, and even more so in everyone who did it.

Sometimes the untapped strength of a company is right there in front of you disguised as that battered ball. Often you can find true value in your company just by asking your own employees how to 're-tape' that ball. I promise you, you'll be amazed at the answers you'll hear and from people that are right there, doing the job, and already working for you. They may even show you a way to buy a new Ball.

Basic Playground stuff!

TEN: NO GIRLS EVER, NO-WAY, NO-HOW

(THIS RULE WAS THE MOST IMPORTANT)

I heard Jeannie passed you a note in school today
.... that's a dirty lie!!!

Time is eventually the master of all things and the Playground was no exception. When boys got to be about twelve years old they started to notice girls. This was particularly distasteful and disgusting to the younger guys who couldn't ever imagine this happening to them.

The neighborhood girls also knew what was happening to these boys and would linger outside the Playground, just beyond the gate. I was lucky to know a very wise black man named Link, who used to do gardening for my Grandmother. Link once told me that the difference between little girls and little boys is that "little girls know they're women, before little boys know they're men". This became painfully evident to us between the ages of twelve and fourteen.

The girls always seemed to be sharing some secret and they were constantly giggling at things we didn't think were very funny. We were always confused around them and even today, that feeling has never totally gone away. They intrigued, attracted, and repulsed us all at the same time. The older boys, those fourteen and fifteen, were not always at the Playground anymore. They spent much of their time at the corner drug store soda fountain, or standing in front of Pete Hatch's Toy Store .

Talking to girls (YUCK)!

They never brought those girls to the Playground though, as that would have been violating a most coveted rule. They now knew something about girls that we didn't, and they knew we weren't capable of understanding it yet. Even still, they would never bring them inside the fence, or put us in the wretched position of having to **play with girls!** This would have violated the basic tenets of Playground honor. These teenage boys now had something in their lives more interesting to them than the Playground. God forbid! They still respected the

'Ladder' though, and having now climbed to the top rung they realized that the rest of us still had a ways to go.

They were now the absentee top dogs at the Playground and had earned their rite of passage. We didn't blame them for it, we just missed them when they weren't there. They had earned our admiration and loyalty even though we couldn't really understand what they were doing now. In spite of this, we still respected the fact that they knew something we didn't. We also knew that they would always be there for us if we needed them. They had left the Playground for girls and later cars, but their Playground experience would endure, sustaining them in many ways for the rest of their lives.

> *Girls had their place ....it was on the other side of the fence*

CHAPTER TWENTY ONE: THE FOURTH OF JULY

Going, going, it was gone, and for the third year in a row, Tommy had won the batting title.

The Fourth of July Holiday Parade was celebrated inside our Playground. This was the only day during the entire year that our parents and neighbors joined with us to celebrate on our turf. This was our Superbowl, World Series, and Stanley Cup all rolled up into one. The Fourth of July was a day of contests, and it was in front of the parents and adults. Bragging rights for the entire year were at stake, and this was serious stuff!

There were races to see who was fastest, throwing contests to see whose was farthest and foul shooting to see who could make the most without a miss. The most coveted event though, was the batting title. The kid who could hit the ball farthest, when pitched to by one of the Fathers, was the top dog. He was the head honcho and unofficial king of our ball-field for an entire year. There could be only one!

As special as this one day was, it had an almost otherworldly feel. We all knew that as much fun as the Fourth of July was, our haven and sanctuary wasn't really a Playground on that day. It was an extension of our homes, and our schools and churches, because all of the neighborhood adults were there. Tomorrow though, the Playground would be returned to us. The innocence and order would be back, with just a few more Fourth of July legends carved into its trees.

It was carved into the tree.

It seems much of the connection to our past has now been cut and lies drifting and dormant. We need to go back and reconnect with those things that were important in shaping who we are. If we really want richness and fulfillment in our lives, we need to reexamine the fundamentals that we were built on, and apply them to our lives today. The Fourth of July is truly a great day of celebration, but on the Playground we celebrated every day! We didn't set just one day aside to do it!

Playgrounds in some form have been around since the dawn of time but were not institutionalized until the first part of the twentieth century. They have created lasting impressions inside the Men who were lucky enough to spend their boyhoods there. Deep within the Playgrounds Web, lessons were learned and characters were formed in an intricate, intuitive and natural manner. These lessons were far from the media-generated and artificial influences that we have today. In the Playground, there was a sense to everything, and everything made sense.

To be totally objective, everything that happened wasn't always good. Occasionally, bad things could and did happen, like the day two of us broke our legs jumping from the hayloft in the old barn. The 'Muse' that controlled and ruled within the Playground though, was overridingly good, with its constant message that tomorrow would be even better. When the rare bad thing did happen, we recognized it for what it was .... bad! No confusion, no misunderstanding, we knew it was bad and we tried to keep it from happening again. It was that simple! The Fourth of July was the one time during the entire year that we got to share this positive message with our parents and family. We only hoped that the weather would be good.

We had the Playground Gods to see to that!

In the Playground we rarely looked back, that was reserved for rainy days. There was just too much to look forward to! Looking back was reserved for hero worship, eulogizing heroes and legends of the past, and of course celebrating our nation's birthday. The Lessons we learned here were taught nowhere else. The professors were varied and the degrees honorary, but the knowledge we gained was eternal.

Company's should celebrate and memorialize events also. Whether it be a 'Founders Day' celebration, a charity fund-raiser, or a recently won civic award. They can all be critical and important to the company's 'Mission Statement,' but first someone has to make them so.

Things that are beyond measure earn more than just
money .... they inspire!

CHAPTER TWENTY TWO: THE LAST ONE CHOSEN

Standing slightly up the hill to look taller, he held his breath. Please, please, pick me now, don't let me be last again.

With great anticipation, ten boys stood in the Playground, five on each side. There were two choosers, captains if you will, usually older boys who picked the players for each team. It started with a coin toss or a throw of fingers, or in baseball season, the last grip at the top of the bat. The idea was to get to choose first. This would have a major effect on the outcome of the game. The other eight boys stood there waiting to be chosen based on ability, size, and proficiency for the game in season. This choosing happened every day and it was about winning. No one wanted to be picked last.

If you were picked last, it was your all-consuming goal to move up to the position of next to last. It was public adulation or humiliation. To that last guy and all the other guys there, it was painfully obvious he had been picked tenth. Even worse, he also knew he might have been picked ninety-ninth, if there had been ninety-nine guys to choose from.

It was a bad spot to be in and you'd do anything to move up. Like five guys running from a lion, you only had to be faster than the slowest guy and that was your goal. Being the smallest or the youngest and getting picked last was no dishonor; we had all been there at one time or another. Being the tallest or biggest kid available, and still being picked last though was a tough cross to bear. This lesson of where you fit and how to deal with it, would prepare you for some of life's tougher lessons when the games became real.

In many cases you had to take your pride and satisfaction from just being part of the team, or in reveling in your team members accomplishments. The important thing was that no matter what your ability, you got to play and take part, and you got to do it with your friends; real friends! Later on in life this would not always be true. In Playground games, you gained much of your self worth from the group, and the groups accomplishments. This always made you a better teammate, and ultimately a better person.

The Playground made room for everyone, and everyone was important. Sometimes, like on the day when only five kids showed up to play, ability took a back seat to the fact that you were a body. More than anything it takes bodies to play the game. On those days you got more shots, more chances to handle the ball, and you went home with the feeling that you had personally held up the Playgrounds honor and pride for that day. Patience and waiting your turn were lessons that came naturally. Sometimes timing and opportunity trumped skill and raw ability. If you were there today and I wasn't, it was your day to shine. Today the Playground was smiling directly at you.

And you couldn't help but smile back.

The Playground found real worth in everyone who played there. Can business today say the same thing? Sometimes, a persons true worth only surfaces in an atmosphere of acceptance and opportunity. How many company workers are ever given this chance? The most effective improvements and change often come from the inside. An overlooked workforce is many times the best instrument of that! Make time to ask your 'B' players what they think.

They may just improve your 'A' game.

Sometimes Old School is best!

CHAPTER TWENTY THREE: SINKING THE BUCKET, REACHING HOME, CROSSING THE GOAL LINE

*Hey, Tommy's got band practice and Mack's been
grounded. I guess it's 'ins and outs' again.*

This chapter is about getting what you want. It may not have been obvious to outsiders, but the Playground was all about goal setting. Not the kind of goal setting we have today which is dictated by consensus and an endless stream of meetings. These goals were real 'feel it in your bones' things that we had to do, and we were constantly amending our master-plan on how to do them.

The goals were usually seasonal. In the fall we were always scrounging the neighborhood to get enough guys to play football. In spring for Baseball it was the same. Only rarely did we have enough guys to really play baseball, so we improvised and played a derivative version of baseball that we called 'ins and outs.' You only needed enough players to take the field, and a minimum of three batters, twelve in all. The game allowed you to play a form of baseball, without one-third the normal amount of players.

The game went like this: A batter would take the plate. Since we had no umpire, there were no balls or strikes. If the batter hit the ball and it landed fair, he stayed on base. If it was a fly ball and caught, the player that caught the fly would take his place at bat, and he in turn went to that player's position in the field. If that same batter hit a ground ball and was thrown or tagged out, the player making the throw or placing the tag would get to bat, and the batter again went to that players spot in the field. This kept three players batting at all times. If two out of the three batters were on base, and you were the third batter and couldn't drive one of them home, you were out, and the pitcher got to take your place at bat.

You were in, you were out; does this sound familiar? The minute you were out you focused totally on getting back in, and there were very specific ways to do this. None of them however involved a coach or parent saying 'every kid plays' or 'no cuts', or 'every kid gets to play every position because this is a developmental league.' You set goals to get in, and then back in again when you were out. It all rested on you!

In 'ins and outs' you had to get yourself back in the game, and you wouldn't have had it any other way. No kid ever offered you his spot unless he was being called home for the dentist, or his Grandma was visiting, and you would never take it anyway. This was serious stuff and you had to earn your way back in. Then you were there until you lost it yourself. You constantly had to re-evaluate your plan as to how to get back up to bat. Some days it involved hitting, and some days it was fielding. Sometimes you just needed to be in the right place at the right time to apply the tag.

We could use more flexible systems like this in business today. Respect for the rules, respect for the individual, and all starting with a love of the game. Today the rules of the game seem to change daily. Companies with a foggy or ill-defined corporate culture often flounder or suffer with every downturn in the business cycle. Many times, they never get back up to bat. They're always looking for a way to steal home. Stealing home wasn't allowed in 'ins and outs.' It was against the rules.

Calls, as to whether you were out or safe, or whether the ball was either fair or foul were worked out through a time-honored tradition of deference and negotiation. **The big guys ruled**! It was basic 'law of the jungle,' and as a young or new guy in the neighborhood you learned first hand to respect your elders, even if they were only two or three years older than you. These things were never questioned because they worked. No petty squabbling, no self-doubts or recriminations, the game (the most important thing) went on. Meetings were held strictly at the discretion of the older guys. No right of appeal, no parents to cry to, the decisions were not only final, but time honored.

After all, our neighborhood was the place where two NFL players, Ted Dean and Emlen Tunnell, and in a nearby Playground one NBA player, Wilt Chamberlain, had learned their stuff. If the rules were good enough for them, they were certainly good enough for us. The only reminders of parental involvement were the bells our Mother's would ring that could be heard for five blocks around, calling us home for dinner.

Of all Playground sports though, basketball was the great unifier. There was something about six, eight, or ten guys all moving together that was unlike all the other sports. Basketball provided a chance (slim I'll admit) for the younger boys to sometimes shine against the older guys. It was all because of 'the shot.' If you had a good shot it sometimes didn't matter how young you were. You just picked your favorite spot, waited for the feed, and let it go. Everyone knew where everyone else's favorite spot was. That was part of your rep, your value to the team, and added to your Playground legacy. Even though you may have been on the other team, you smiled secretly to yourself when Jimmy McGarrity hit that corner jumper that he was so famous for, and Jimmy was only five feet five.

How many times in corporate life do we take the time to recognize our co-workers strength's, their corner jump-shot? If we do, how many of us try to help our associates develop those strengths (box out) to a point where everyone can leverage them and score? How many times do we even give them a chance to shoot? My shot as a young guy was from the far right baseline corner. Unmolested, I would sink it sixty percent of the time. The big guys on my ream would 'box out' the other teams big guys so I could get in position. Wouldn't it be nice in today's corporate world if we did the same? We learned in the Playground that it was about winning the game, not who won it, but did **WE** win!

We played these games with clarity of purpose and religious zeal. There was nothing ambiguous or confusing about the outcome. It was pure. Someone else's reality was on the other side of the fence, but over here, in our Playground, we set goals and we played to win.

And we all knew the score

Nothing ever matched the feeling of that first Bike!

CHAPTER TWENTY FOUR: YOUR BIKE AND RESPECT FOR PROPERTY

Hey, who took the clothespins and baseball cards off the wheels of my bike? Somebody's gonna pay!

More than anything, your bike represented freedom. It was your property and nobody messed with another kid's bike. Your bike allowed you to travel a wider radius, away from your normal sphere of influence and supervision. In many ways, it was a Playground unto itself. The minute you mastered the two-wheeler for the first time you just knew. Your bike was really about one thing: freedom! As great as your car would eventually become, it never quite lived up to that first day the training wheels came off your bike. You were finally free, and you might never experience anything this great ever again.

Stealing someone's bike was like horse stealing in the old west. We all know how serious that was and the punishment it carried. Bike locks were virtually non-existent, and your bike by its personalization, carried your own individual brand. If it went missing, we all went after it. Stealing a kid's bike was the ultimate act of larceny and disrespect. Woe and mayhem to the one who got caught stealing another kid's bike! The Indian ritual of 'running the gauntlet' would be mild punishment compared to what we'd dish out. To put it mildly you'd only steal a bike once.

If you survived the punishment the Playground exacted, the banishment that followed would make your parents feel like they had to move. Your name might never be mentioned in the neighborhood again, and all the other parents in the neighborhood would have agreed. Your first car, as great as it was, never quite 'lived up' to the total freedom you felt on your bike.

In business, stealing someone's marketing plan, sales forecast or customer, should come with the same punishment. It stems from a serious character flaw, and a total lack of respect for fair play. We talk about having these virtues, but many times it's just talk. Respect flows both ways and it usually comes back bigger than it went out. Not all ideas are good ideas, but respect for the individual behind the idea should be preserved, even when the idea is not. If the Bike broke or lost a part, our best and usually most cost effective option was to fix it, not throw it away.........

And we did!

People deserve at least the same consideration. In our disposable society, everyone and everything seems to eventually get tossed. The rules of today's games, ethics, and codes of behavior frequently get tossed too. Chaos, confusion, and low morale usually are the end result.

Learn to recognize the other guy's bike, then treat it like your own!

The branch (Wilt) had been trimmed back but still threatens

CHAPTER TWENTY FIVE: SYMBOLS, NICKNAMES, AND THE MEANINGS THEY HOLD

Rat a tat tooey, the Rat sunk a 30 footer again!

Not only did we all have nicknames that were the results of positive, negative, and embarrassing events in our Playground life, we also named many of the inanimate objects that resided in the Playground. Whether it was the baseball backstop, the bent rim on the north-side backboard, or the tree branch that hung down over the south side court, we named them all.

The backstop behind home plate had five holes in it and we called it 'the sieve'. Every kid knew as he was rounding second base and heading toward third, that if the throw to the plate went through one of those holes in the back of the backstop, everyone would come safely home and score. By the time the catcher ran around behind the backstop, down the hill, and into the creek to retrieve the ball, we all could have tagged home-plate and gone to Nick Samuelson's for a Soda and still have been back before he'd return with that wet ball, and that's 'IF' he could find it.

The bent rim on the basketball court was called Leaning Leroy and made it possible for some of us to dunk long before our time. Every time a kid tried to dunk and hit that rim, it bent some more, and hung down just a little lower in the front. By the time I left the Playground, it was closer to vertical than horizontal. It never dawned on any of us to try and fix it. It was just part of the Playground and we adapted our game around it. It was fruitless for any kid from another playground to challenge us on that end of the court.

We all had 'Leaning Leroy' wired, and we accepted this as one of several challenges unique to our Playground.. Actually we highlighted it and gave it special reverence, turning a potential negative into a playground icon. How much corporate effort gets tossed in the wastebasket because no-one can see or cares to search for the positives hidden behind a surface problem?

The tree branch hanging over the south end of the court we called 'Wilt'. This was in tribute to the great Wilt Chamberlain. Wilt had gone to Overbrook High School in West Philadelphia and then on to the University of Kansas. Wilt also played in the N.B.A. for the 76'ers and the Lakers. We named the branch Wilt because of its length and shape. Wilt was over seven feet tall and the branch looked just like his giant arm coming down from overhead, settling not more than six or eight feet above the backboard and rim. You couldn't put your normal arc on your shot at this end of the court. 'Wilt' would block it for sure.

You had to adopt a new shot to deal with 'Wilt,' and you eventually became as good at this end of the court with your flat shot, as you were at the other end with your arc. Did it ever occur to us to climb that tree and saw off that branch? NO WAY! 'Wilt' was as much a part of the Playground as we were and he was treated with a reverence from those of us that had to shoot under or around him. 'Wilt' was just another defining obstacle on the way to becoming a Man, and we loved calling out his name in frustration when he would silently block another shot that had just a little too much arc.

Many of life's challenges are like this. They're different from the paradigms, or what we read about in the company instruction books or manuals. 'Wilt' wasn't there when they first built that basketball court, and the backstop wasn't put up with holes in it either. These are natural occurrence's in life. To be successful, we have to adjust and adapt our games to deal with them. How many people do you know or work with that go ballistic when things just aren't like they're supposed to be in the company guide book?

I know these people would have benefited from more time on the Playground. My pal's Grinchy, Big Guy, the Moose, Neemo, Jackson, Tommy O', Pepe, Reds, Mack, Rat, and Fleetfoot certainly did.

When you nickname an obstacle, you bond with that challenge and it becomes part of you. When you nickname a person, you celebrate his individuality in a way many no longer understand. Many indigenous tribes start life with one name, only to be renamed based on events or accomplishment's as they grow older.

Native Americans will also tell you that much of a tribe's greatness is measured by how powerful its enemies are. In the Playground we knew this instinctively, and took a personal pride in every roadblock and pothole and wore its badge proudly.

If it mattered, it was on the Tree.

CHAPTER TWENTY SIX: CARVE IT ON THE TREE

Extra, extra, read all about it! Has anybody got a knife?

If it was really worth remembering, it was probably worth carving on the tree. We had a giant maple tree at the end of our park that was almost entirely covered with the names and dates of our Playground history. If you hit three homeruns on July second, it was on there. If you put a caterpillar down Jeannie Hutch's back as she cut through the Playground on her way to Girl Scouts, it was on there too. The entire history of our Playground was written on that maple tree, and if you were really lucky like I was, thirty years later you could climb that tree with your own son, and retell those stories again. Maybe you could even carve his name under yours.

The history of my era is now about fifteen feet above the ground. Like all stories and deeds of past accomplishments, that's the way it should be. Our history is still there, it's just taller and higher, kind of like the stories we now tell of our glory days in the park. That old tree just needed to move us up and make room for the accomplishments of a new generation of Playground all-stars, just in case a new generation ever shows up. Those carvings high up in the tree immortalize the richness of the experiences we had down below. In the deep recesses of its bark we carved our memories, allowing for a certain poetic license with the truth. What great things that tree must have seen from its towering height. Many afternoons I sat high in her branches, trying to see my future, far beyond the Playground's fence.

In reading the carvings it reminded me that we were much more concerned with the spirit of what had happened, than any boring details. What were a few embellishments, when telling of great deeds from the past? As I read the names of the boys I grew up with, there at the very top, almost beyond reach it said 'Johnny and Kurt 1957'. Many times Johnny and I sat on this very branch and talked about the great things we would do, and how we would do them together. Johnny only lived one more year after we carved our names; I carving his and he carving mine while we both carved the date. I only hope he knows how much he is still with me today and how that inscription is also carved into my heart and my soul. I've missed you every day since you've been gone John.

We carved them often, we carved them deep, and we carved them ourselves!

I know my son loved hearing the stories about the Playground and the guys who played there, and in fact has regaled in retelling these stories to his own friends. I've been lucky enough to hear him do this. Listening to him retell what he heard me say, it's hard to believe he wasn't actually there himself. Maybe he was. He's already promised me he will take his own son and one day climb the great Old Maple. He'll then carve his son's name underneath his Father's and Grandfather's. I hope I live to see that.

Native American's have no real written history. It is almost entirely oral in the form of storytelling, or painted on the sides of teepees and petroglyph rock paintings. I think maybe they got it right. Important things should be passed down to ensuing generations that way. Whether it's from father to son, friend to friend, or older boy to younger boy, that tradition just seems to mean so much more.

That old tree symbolizes a rite and celebration of passage that sadly no longer exists. The bottom ten feet of the tree is now bare except for a few vulgar and profane markings, symbolizing what much of adolescence has become. We didn't need the direct supervision of adults to evolve, or to tell us what to do minute by minute, and then tell us whether we were any good or not. We had the Playground for that. Our parents were busy working and keeping house for us, and we respected and loved them for that. We also had our own serious work to do and that was the business of being kids. We were all kids who belonged to our Playground, which belonged to our community, and in turn our state and country. We were all connected, and we knew it.

And we would all be forever remembered in our
Playground Wall Street Journal................
the Giant Maple!

If we ever forgot, we just had to go read it on the tree! The tree was a living, breathing thing that held our stories. Year after year as the tree grew, our stories got taller too with their retelling. It was the pride behind the stories that provided the richness. Corporations could also benefit from a 'company tree', one that their employees could rally around and feel a pride and kinship with. Their tree could hold their stories. Our tree belonged to everyone and no one at the same time. Like many things in the Playground, it was bigger than that!

And so were most of the people immortalized in her bark!

CHAPTER TWENTY SEVEN: PETE'S TOY AND HOBBY SHOP

Weather Forecast: Rain all day. *Great, meet you at Pete's*

On the rare occasion when not enough boys would show up to play because of rain or snow, we all migrated to Pete's. His Toy Shop had a gravitational pull on us greater than the earths over the moon. Pete's was two blocks away from the Playground, but it was like the finger way out there on the end of your arm: a distance away but still connected. Pete loved us and we loved him. From balsa wood windup airplanes, to super yo-yo's, Pete had them all and he let us play with them. It truly had a vacation feel every time you entered his shop.

Pete was the quartermaster of our dreams

Pete told us where all the contractors in the neighborhood were working, so we could go and collect their empty soda bottles and redeem them, two cents for a regular soda bottle, and five for the quart size. A dime back then got you half way to buying something really good. It would buy you a soda, cupcakes or the Holy Grail, a pack of fresh baseball cards. Every kid was on the perennial hunt for a Mickey Mantle or Willie Mays rookie card, or maybe the rare minor league insert. We would trade them, flip them in competition, but always covet them. You almost never flipped your great cards, the one's you couldn't afford to loose. This was like a company putting its working capital at risk. They were the lifeblood of your collection; and unless you were having a momentary loss of sanity, you didn't gamble with them.

To flip cards, each boy would hold a card flat in his hand at waist height. He would then drop and flip the card at the same time, spinning it sideways as it fell to the ground. If you called even and both cards landed either face or backside up, you won. If one of the cards landed, showing the stats. side up, and the other face side, you lost. It was an early lesson in risk-management. You knew beforehand what you were willing to loose. You might even have doubles, or excess inventory of some cards, which allowed you to push your position based on your current resources. Those cards were our currency, our stocks and bonds. The kid that got reckless and lost an Ernie Banks or Hank Aaron would sulk for days, and have to take the wrath written in our Wall Street Journal; the Giant Maple. The embarrassment was now permanent, and carved in its legacy forever.

It was a lesson you didn't forget

Pete's form of advertising was word of mouth, and he even directed you to the financing. It sometimes took a week to cash in enough bottles to buy that super squirt gun, but it was always worth it. We set goals, we planned our strategy, and we hit our targets. Sometimes the construction workers would even pay us to run to 'Nicks' and get them soda's, letting us keep the empty bottles after they drank them. On really hot days, if we got to the store and back quickly, they even let us keep the change from the money they gave us. We became an invaluable part of the local supply chain, and all with an end in sight. Those construction workers were great guys, and liked seeing boys being industrious, while all the while engaged in 'free-play.'

Pete Hutch's Toy and Hobby Shop was our first vacation home. It was a place to go and break the routine. Like a tropical Island, the weather was always good inside Pete's. Pete was wise, and always gave us options and optimism when the situation looked bleak. Pete was our Peter Drucker, our 'Father of Modern Management.'

CHAPTER TWENTY EIGHT: THE PLAY-GROUND WAS NOT ALWAYS KIND

*Running as fast as he could, he made the mistake of
looking back. This slowed him just enough to get caught
by the Playground's assailants*

As welcoming as the Playground was, you had to meet a certain minimum standard to walk through the gate. The Playground was close to perfect in its democracy, but it couldn't always perform miracles. Some boy's, and there were only a few, just couldn't muster up the right stuff. You had to be able to cut the apron strings with Mom, if just for a little while, to come to the Playground. It was an unwritten rule: Mom's weren't allowed in. Some boy's just couldn't do it. My cousin Teddy was one of them.

Teddy and his family lived in a town eighty miles to the north of us. Teddy was as nice a kid as you could ever hope to meet, and just slightly older than I was. This made us more like brothers than cousins. The problem was that Teddy was filled with fear; and as hard as I tried, I could never make that go away.

His fear was the result of a highly overprotective Mother, who did everything for him from the day he was born. My Aunt protected him from everything. When he was a Toddler learning to walk and it looked like he might stumble and fall, she was always right there to keep him upright. Her answer to his being afraid of the dark at night was to let Teddy sleep with her. When other kid's learned to swim at the local pool, she told Teddy the water was too cold, or too deep, so he stayed in the baby pool. Teddy's 'training wheels' never came off the two-wheeler that my parents bought him for his eighth birthday. He still lives at home with his eighty-eight year old Mother today. He never married, or started a life of his own, the training wheels of his life still firmly in place.

How can you ever get in the fast lane, if your training wheels never come off?

When Teddy's Mom and Dad finally bought their dream house, it was right across the street from the Huntley Avenue Playground. I couldn't wait to go and visit, as we often did. We would then embark on the many adventures that a new Playground, in a new town, with a whole new cast of squirts and legends would provide. I had one major problem though, my cousin Teddy would not go into that Playground. He was always hesitant about coming into my Playground when his family came to visit us. He only did it because he knew I was a fixture there, and all the guys inside were my very best friends. They treated Teddy the way they treated me. He was my cousin, and family mattered!

His new Playground on Huntley Avenue though was a different story. His Mom, my Aunt Ellen, explained to me that when they first moved into the neighborhood Teddy tried to take his younger sister Liz, who was three years younger than he was, into the Playground to use the swings and gym equipment. This equipment was something that my Playground had too, but we thought it was only for babies, or God forbid, girls. We would never go near it. That stuff was for the real little guys when their parents were with them on the weekends. We wouldn't have been caught dead swinging on the swings, or sliding down that sliding board, even if we secretly wanted to. The only time you saw parents in our Playground was when they brought their toddlers to use the swing-sets, or to play in the sandbox in the late evenings and weekends. We treated that end of the Playground like it had the plague, suitable only for toddlers and dare I say it again, G-I-R-L-S.

Some Playground rules truly were universal

His Mom then explained to me that a group of 'toughs' started making fun of Teddy and teasing his little sister. Instead of trying to stand up for himself and his little sister Liz, Teddy chose to run, leaving his little sister behind. This is practically a death sentence socially for any new kid trying to enter the world of any neighborhood Playground for the first time. His 'right stuff' had been measured and he was found lacking. At this point he was almost certainly doomed to a life outside the gate. Outside the gate didn't work for me. I desperately wanted and needed what was happening inside. On our first visit to Teddy's new house, I insisted that he and I go to the Playground together to see what was going on. He came up with every excuse imaginable not to go, but I wasn't buying it. I literally dragged him into that Park. Once there, I asked him if he could point out who the boys were that had verbally accosted he and his sister. He was very reluctant to do this, but my consistent prodding finally won out.

The boys in question were in the middle of a three-on-three basketball game, so we took a seat and watched. It took only a minute for one of the boys to say something derogatory to Teddy, and by association, to me. Let's just say this kid only said it once. I handled it the way you handled things in any Playground. It was quick, it was final, and it was over. On that day there was now a new sense of social acceptance in the Huntley Avenue Playground, if only a temporary one. For three more days we played, joked, and hung out with all the guys there. It was great fun, and I really hated to go home.

That was when the trouble returned for Teddy

The next day after we had left, Teddy tried going into the Playground by himself. The boys were waiting for him. If they had no reason to tease and abuse him initially, they felt totally justified now. Their Playground honor had been challenged by an outsider, me, and they were now going to set things right. Teddy received his first bloody nose that day because he just couldn't run fast enough. Of course Teddy's Mother responded by locking him 'safely' inside the house, where no further harm could happen to him. When I heard what happened, I realized it had been my fault. I only had the best of intentions, but what's that old adage about the 'pathway to hell being paved.........'

Sometimes the greatest harm to ourselves, happens from the inside out

To my knowledge, Teddy never entered that Playground, or any Playground ever again. If he had fought back, his nose already bloodied, I know in time those boys would have accepted him as one of their own. How can a kid that won't even try to stand up for himself or his Sister, be expected to represent their Playground? He couldn't. I often think that if his Mom had let those training wheels fall off when he was five or six, his knees and elbows may have gotten a little bloody, but his confidence and character would have been just fine.

Anything except themselves!

My cousin Teddy's story is not unique and unfortunately got played out all across America. It was the Playgrounds grass roots form of natural selection. Just as in the old adage it's better to 'teach a man to fish, than feed a man a fish,' on many days in the Playground you had to be able to stand on your own. If you paid attention and put in your time, the Playground would eventually show you the way, but the basic raw material needed to be there first. On the few occasions when challenged you got the chance to show what you were really made of. You couldn't use your out-of-town cousin for protection when he was no longer there. I learned a valuable lesson that day too. You can save most people from almost anything, anything that is except themselves! This also includes fatally bad parenting, no matter how well intended. Good Parenting = Good Playground Experience = Good School and Work Experience!

Sounds simple doesn't it, but based on recorded history, that's how it usually worked! The Playground was very forgiving, but you didn't get a free pass. There had to be some form of the right stuff within you to begin with. Then the playground could really work its magic. Parents had to do their jobs too when you were very young. Then you could walk confidently and hopefully through that Playground gate; alone! Some guys, and there were very few, just didn't measure up.

Companies and corporations need a minimum standard too. Quota's and hiring mandates are fine on paper, but they often result in the wrong person doing the wrong job. These workers are often unqualified and chosen just because they fill a state or national hiring statute on that day.

The no-cut and everyone plays Little League teams of today perpetuate the weaknesses that the 'free-play' environment of the Playground filtered out. Its merit-based system weeded out those that would never cut it. Corporations need to look at the big picture and do the same. I love my cousin Teddy, but he'll never belong to anything bigger or better than himself. He'll never be confident enough to hold a position of responsibility, or to make decisions involving the futures of someone or something else.

He can't even do that for himself

'Who's really in charge here?'

'Jeesh Dad, you're awful Big !'

CHAPTER TWENTY NINE: THE EXPERTS, AND THE PARENT SURROGATES, ALL FOR A FEE

Circa 2008: The count is 3-0 and there are runners on first and second base. Kevin's big chance to shine has finally come. Instead of swinging away he calls timeout and walks over to the fence and asks his Father what to do.

We would often share our stories of conquest and glory with our parents at the dinner table. They would laugh and revel in our exaggerations of our Playground exploits. They constantly told us we could be whatever we wanted to be, but it was the Playground however that showed us how. Our Playground's were the temples of our growth, and they were the centers of our lives between the ages of eight and fifteen.

Once you started to discover girls and eventually drive, a transition to another place started. The lessons you learned and the friends you made though would always be locked safely away in the heart of the Playground. Remember how it felt when you drove by the Playground when you were sixteen, seventeen, or eighteen, and saw the guys, some of them your guys, practicing the time-honored ritual of 'climbing the ladder'. Tell me you didn't smile and remember, just a little.

Today's parent-dominated play environment, with its professional babysitters, (coaches, trainers, camp counselors, summer interns etc.)

is masked as 'free-play', but it isn't. Parent's hearts are in the right place, but unfortunately their children aren't. As a father myself, I totally understand the safety concerns of parents not wanting to leave their children unsupervised in this modern era of crime, drugs, and sometimes child predation. These things are real and need to be dealt with. Sadly, the baby has been thrown out with the bath water. The cost we are paying is the total annihilation of 'free-play,' in an environment where children had most of the control, allowing them to grow independent, creative, and strong.

Now we have Kids that can run faster and jump higher, but in many cases have no idea where they're running to. They see life in very small increments, suffering with maladies like A.D.D & A.D.H.D. Their Video Game and MTV environment has replaced a wonderland where they used to make up the games, and the rules for how to play them. The first thing my kids pediatrician said right after they were born was "get them with kids their own age, and then let them play."

When I asked him to explain he said, 'barring them hurting each other, let the babies play together and work things out on their own." Dr. Edward Troncellitti was one of the wisest men I've ever known.

Experts talk about the social effects and aftermath of the modern depravations that endanger America's Youth. However, I don't think they will ever be able to measure the effect of things that never got a chance to happen. Things like personality traits, leadership ability, and character, only fully develop in an atmosphere of Free-Play. If you could buy those traits with money, America with its riches would be problem free, but you can't. Character, real character, has the properties of a diamond. It is formed over time and under pressure. The time was natural and the pressure came from the Playground. Store bought substitutes, the damage of too much T.V., and the effects of surrogate parenting all fall far short of the mark.

It's hard to 'think on your feet' in a business environment, when you've spent almost your entire adolescence sitting on your @$$

It may not have been exclusive, but it was as close to heaven as we could dream about back then.

CHAPTER THIRTY: THIS AIN'T NO COUNTRY CLUB

He stared longingly out the back window of his Dad's car. He was headed off to the 'Country Club' again, missing the nightly 'Wiffle-Ball' game with the guys.

The Playground was not a country club. There was no price of admission, or exclusive standards necessary to be admitted. You could be black, white, red or yellow. It didn't matter. What did matter was how you played, and how you fit into the group. You may have been a social outcast or juvenile delinquent outside the playground, and yes we had a few, but what really mattered was how you acted inside the fence.

In 1958 my Parents joined the local country club. Being a young, upwardly mobile couple, and enjoying the success of my Fathers growing business, my parents decided that this was one way in which they could celebrate. I hated it! Not because I didn't like the people there, or didn't want to learn to play golf. It was because it took time away from my favorite place, the Playground. After dinner in the summers, my parents would hurry up and clear the table, and then head to the *'club'* with us kids in tow to get in nine holes. This of course meant that I had to miss the nightly 'Wiffle-Ball' game in the street. I would then have to suffer through the entire next day hearing who hit twelve home runs, and who threw who out trying to make it home. It just wasn't fair. How could a country club ever compare to a 'Wiffle-Ball' game, or the Playground? It couldn't. Not then, and not now. The country club was stuffy to a ten-year old, and the country club had strange rules. Most of them seemed to be about what you *couldn't* do.

A direct opposite from the Playground

How we go from the inclusive nature of our nation's Playgrounds, to the exclusive practices of our golf, tennis and yacht clubs is probably the subject for another book and another writer. I am just so grateful that my earliest experiences were on a grass field surrounded by a chain link fence. It was inside that fence that I felt the Playground wrap its four acre/arms around me, and knowing that feeling was good.

How we develop the later prejudices of black/white, democrat/republican, or any choice at the exclusion of another, is not something we learned there. We had to fit in and find a way to adapt to one another. The weather and the big guys called all the shots. That's the way it was, and that was A-OK with us. It worked because at different ages, and at different times, we all got to be squirts, then decent players, and finally the big guys.

It was fair, even when it was unfair

If that doesn't make sense to you, then you probably didn't grow up in a Playground where the whole truly was greater than the sum of its parts. There were no polo ponies or alligators on our shirts symbolizing our dreams. We lived them every day, and we lived them together!

CHAPTER THIRTY ONE: VIOLENT BUT NOT WITH YOU

The stare-down was over. Joe took the first punch but delivered the second, then five more. To his credit, Bobby was still on his feet, but the fight was over.

The Playground's resident tough guy could be violent, but he almost never directed this towards you. Not unless you were dumb enough to challenge his honor, by publicly embarrassing him, or making him look like a fool in front of the other guys. Then the punishment was swift, like being shown the door after making the company look bad because of a dumb comment you made at the quarterly board-meeting. Nothing was more fundamental or learned earlier, than the recognition of power.

The young neighborhood girls sensed this more than anyone, and it harkened back to Robert Bly's 'Iron John,' "Men are attractive because of their fierceness." The Playground took on an aura proportional to its 'tough guy status' not unlike many corporations. The tough guys roles were limited but invaluable when called upon. He was the Playground's last line of defense, even though his role was mostly one of deterrence. Similar to many companies, the tough guy's role was usually passed down from the resident champion to his heir apparent, sometimes willingly, and sometimes not.

The mechanics of this process were mostly known only to the tough guys, but it gave the Playground the stability and the security it needed. In the movie *'A Few Good Men'* Jack Nicholson, while under interrogation from Tom Cruise says, "Somewhere in places you don't admit, you want me on that wall, where four thousand Cubans try to kill me before breakfast." He then finishes it with the immortal line,

"You want the truth, you can't handle the truth." In our Playground, the truth was governed by principles based on natural selection and the Law of the Jungle. Bobby Gross was our resident Tarzan. As the movie above portrayed, he also made sure none of our weaker boys were picked on or abused.

Bobby was from the poor side of our town and was almost sixteen in the eighth grade. He had been ruling our four-acre domain for as long as anyone could remember. Even when we were much younger, Bobby still seemed so much bigger and older than we were. It wasn't only his age that made him the resident tough guy. Bobby earned and retained this title due to the several times when he had successfully defended his crown. These events, though seldom, were major occurrences in the Playground and were attended like a championship bout. They almost never happened by accident and were full of anticipation and bravado. The challenge usually came from another playground, and we were all extremely proud of Bobby when he successfully defended our honor.

Bobby almost retired undefeated. At sixteen, just about everyone leaves the Playground for the world of cars and girls. I say almost because of Joe Church. Joe was a Navy brat whose Dad was an Admiral at the Philadelphia Navy Yard. They had just moved up from Norfolk Virginia, and one gray thursday afternoon Joe showed up on the Playground for the first time. No words had to be exchanged, or threats made, it was just something you knew. Bobby and Joe knew it better than anyone. There could only be one Playground 'numero uno,' and today there would be a changing of the guard.

Like Bobby but even more so, Joe was advanced physically for his age. He was very athletic and muscular. He had an air of quiet defiance, bred by years of moving from one navy town to the next, having to defend his honor at every stop. No one quite remembers exactly how the fight started. Someone heard the word 'punk' shouted and it began. It was over almost as quickly as it started. Joe pinned Bobby up against the chain link backstop and beat him to a pulp with less than six punches. This kid could really fight. It's funny though; with Joe there was no bravado or posturing, just a raging controlled fury that you hoped would never be directed toward you. Joe was later highly decorated in Viet Nam, and all of us who shared our waning years at the Playground with him were very proud, including Bobby Gross.

Another Playground legend was made!

Most corporations have their resident tough guy, or gal. You can only hope that they got their training, and cut their teeth, on the grass and asphalt of a distant Playground. That way you can be sure that their lessons were true. If not, you may have to suffer the rants and tirades of some Donald Trump or Jack Welch wannabee. The real tough guys pass their strength along in the form of confidence and security to those working under them, just like Bobby and Joe did for us. This creates an atmosphere of stability and confidence that allows everyone to thrive and prosper. This again comes from lessons truly learned and paid for. The God's of the Playground instilled this. They entered your soul on the fields and courts of adolescence.

And they never leave!

CHAPTER THIRTY TWO: THE KID WHO WATCHED FROM HIS WINDOW

Like an armchair quarterback, Stanley yelled taunts from the safety of his bedroom window, too afraid to join in.

Watching from the window, lessons can only be observed but never learned. How to form the perfect pocket in your mitt, how to choose up sides when an odd number of guys show up, or how to look a kid in the eye and know he's going to go to war over a foul on the basketball court, these things can only be learned 'inside the fence.'

The absolute dejection you feel after just loosing your 'Willie Mays' card, flipping for your buddies 'Mickey Mantle,' is a hands-on visceral thing. It's something you can't experience second or third hand, you just had to be there. Looking back, you now realize that your first business meetings were held up on top of the batting cage, or behind the big rock over the creek, celebrated by those first cigarettes, hidden in that special place known only to the trusted few. All of these things could only be felt and learned by participation.

Spectating just didn't cut it!

There was one kid on our street, Stanley, who never came inside the park. His house bordered the east end of the Playground, and every day he would watch from the other side of his dark bedroom window. Like many of the 'armchair' quarterbacks in business today, he made sarcastic comments from the relative safety of his bedroom window that he would never have made inside the fence. There, he had mommy to protect him. He never felt the rush or the risk involved with a great Playground victory. He never engaged. Worst of all, he never really became part of something bigger than himself. I often wonder if he still carries the feeling of opportunities lost within him today. He had an open invitation, but like the turtle he chose to stay inside his shell where it was safe but also dark.

I'm sure inside there, he was both lonely and alone

What percentage of potentially valued company employees are like Stanley, off on the sidelines and afraid to contribute? Whether their reluctance stems from fear of criticism, or an inability to function within a group, one thing is almost certainly true; they never spent much time inside a Playground.

The only window should be the window of opportunity!

CHAPTER THIRTY THREE:
THANKSGIVING DINNER AND THE
SHOES OF OUR HERO'S

As good as my Grandmother's coleslaw and stuffing was,
I could hear the yelling coming from beyond the fence.
The game had begun.

After Dinner on Thanksgiving Day and feeling a little bloated, we headed right back to the Playground. It was a four-day weekend, and we weren't going to waste a minute of it. Some of us hid desserts under our jackets, and shared them with some of the other guy's whose Mom's didn't cook so well.

Thanksgiving Dinner at most American tables was a time of remembrance, nostalgia, and gratitude. At our table there was thankfulness, spiced with a heavy dose of nostalgia and stories from the past. This made me want to get back to the Playground even more. As I listened to my Uncle's and Grandparents talk about their pasts, with emotion in their voices rarely heard at other times, I knew I wanted to get back to the business of creating my own stories. I wanted to get on with creating the tales I would tell to my own grandchildren one day, at my Thanksgiving table. As Mom was serving up the great Thanksgiving feast, the Playground was serving up a four-day dream.

It was usually cool on these late November afternoons, just perfect for us budding Jim Browns and Paul Hornungs to recreate the glory we had seen them perform on our little black and white TV's. We loved the sound of the leaves crackling beneath our 'Chuck Taylor All-Stars', as we moved in athletic harmony, we boys of autumn. If a pass was dropped or a ball got fumbled, it was always blamed on forgetting to wear your 'Chuck's.' You might also complain that you outgrew your old 'Chuck's,' and your Mom hadn't taken you to get new one's yet. Many of us had to pay for our own out of the money we earned cutting grass or delivering our paper routes. That made them even more special. I put mine on top of my dresser at night, which was just to the right of the window in my bedroom looking out on the Playground. I would lay in bed and *dream* of the spectacular athletic feats I had yet to accomplish. In the waning light, and by the glow of the moon outside my window, those sneakers seemed to come alive.

If you we're really lucky, a favorite aunt like my Aunt Ellen might come to visit on Thanksgiving. Then you might just get a card with a little money in it, enough money to buy a new pair of 'Chucks.' All the guys wore Chuck Taylor's because that's what the greats wore. Bob Cousy of the Boston Celtics, and our own Wilt Chamberlain of the Philadelphia Warriors wore 'Chuck's.' We might not have the same shooting percentage or free throw average as our NBA heroes, but at least we got to wear the same shoes that they did. Back then, wearing the state of the art in athletic footwear would set you back about eight dollars. Compare that to the mega-buck shoes of today. Most are only fashion statements that never see a court or field, touchdown or homerun. Many of these expensive shoes are just testaments to posturing, profiling, and what might have been.

'Chuck's' were like wings, carrying us to run faster, jump higher, and juke and dodge more precisely than ever before. They weren't flashy or pretentious, and they only came in two colors, tan and black. My Mother would never let me wear black because, just like in the cowboy movies, she said good guys always wore white.

But I always wanted a black pair!

Profiling and superficiality didn't last long in the Playground. That was for the James Dean and Elvis impersonators that hung out in front of the corner drug store. These so-called tough guys were almost always humbled in gym class at school for their lack of any athletic skill or even worse, a willingness to try. Their leather jackets and engineer boots couldn't help them when Mr. Visalio, our beloved gym teacher who we all called Mr. V, would say 'line up.' That's when they usually made some excuse to try and get out of playing in whatever game Mr. V. had picked for that day. Dodge ball was our favorite because we all got to see these self-declared tough guys run like girls as we careened those volleyball's off their heads and other vulnerable areas. In our Chuck Taylor All-Stars, we dreamed the vicarious dreams of hero worshipping kid's. These dreams would become the foundation for all later success.

We believed in our dreams, and we believed we could make them happen.

We dreamed because there was real magic attached to them. Paul Hornung and Wilt Chamberlain understood why we dreamed because they had dreamed too. We were sure of that!

While much of our family was still sitting and reminiscing around the Thanksgiving table, our dessert was the richest of all. We were feasting on the dessert that only 'free-play' can serve up.

The Playground dream!

How many companies today dare to dream or reward their employee's for doing so? One of my favorite quotes from literature is "show me a man without a dream, and I will show you no man at all." This is true of companies too. Thanksgiving to a Playground kid was about listening to the dreams of your family, past and present, while knowing your dreams were still in the future.

Just on the other side of that fence!

As good a support system as there ever was.

CHAPTER THIRTY FOUR: THE FRINGES OF THE NEIGHBORHOOD

Like giant arms they surrounded us, holding us safe in their embrace.

The Playground had a vibe that spread through the houses and alleyways that lined its border. The fence was not able to contain the energy created by the kids who played there. It fanned out and across the Playground's edge to the houses and stores that formed our boundary. The neighbors immediately outside the Playground fed off this energy and took a particular pride in sharing it with us. If we needed water in the summer, or a shovel to get the snow off the courts in the winter, there was always a neighbor along that perimeter to lend a hand. They knew and believed in what we were doing because they had done it themselves. If someone accidentally got hurt in a game or contest, there was a ready supply of 'paramedics' and 'nurses' to come to our aid.

How many real and effective support structures, back up systems, and safety nets do kids have today? There was a direct connection between the people who lived around the Playground and the kids who played in it. The neighbors would often watch us play from their backyard porches. You could see by the looks on their faces that they were being mentally transported back to a time when they were again playing too. This was the connection we shared. I'm afraid today that connection has been broken. They watched over and protected the process that allowed us to grow. They protected it because they understood its value, and they loved and believed in what it would ultimately represent!

These neighbors grew up and had to trade their Playground games for the reality of a life outside the fence. That time would eventually come for everyone, but not without them leaving a big part of themselves behind, behind and *inside* the fence. We represented that part of them now, and they could relive it, if only in a small way, through us. Their houses and businesses that surrounded the Playground were our constant security blanket. There only if we needed them.

But they were always there!

'Would most even have the nerve to enter'

Abandoned, and where some kid's are forced to play

CHAPTER THIRTY FIVE: PHILADELPHIA CORNERS AND THE INTERSECTION YOU WERE FROM

Yo! Just tell me the street corner

The inner-city playgrounds of Philadelphia were often known by the name of an intersection. Broad and Erie, Kensington and Allegheny, and Eighth and Race were street corner intersections where inner-city boys from Philadelphia played and pursued their rites of passage toward manhood. These intersections were every bit as beloved to them as our sylvan suburban Playground's were to us. It may only have been asphalt or concrete, and the sport may have been played with half a tennis ball thrown at a broom handle, but the lesson's learned were the same. The memories were just as cherished too, if not more so.

These lessons and the experiences they shared bonded life-long friendships and were exactly the same as at any field or park. Here, the expectations for the future may have been tempered by a harder reality, but dreams were still dreams. These denizens of half-ball and stickball were sometimes even more creative, coming away with even better results than their suburban counterparts.

The inner city kids had less to lose and everything to gain. Whether it was Bill Cosby, Geraldo Rivera or Robert De Niro, the inner-city's of America produced some of the best.

Things and people were much closer to each other in the city and this had an effect on the games that were played and the relationship's that formed. A homerun wasn't a 250-foot shot over the left field fence. It was smacking the ball with your fist hard enough to get it to the roof of Mrs. Giordano's house, a half a block away. The baseball-diamond was two cars for first and third base, with a manhole cover in the middle for second. The game's were played with one eye on your opponent and one eye on that car that always seemed to come down the street at exactly the wrong time. Here the Playground may have been smaller, but the friendship's that resulted were as big as on any field. The lesson's learned here were even bigger still!

How many times in today's business world do we get blindsided or surprised by that sudden unforeseen occurrence. These inner city kids were ready for it; in fact it was an everyday part of who they were. Sometimes the police sirens or the fire-truck brought a stark realism to the lightheartedness of the games, but in time it all got managed and it all became commonplace. Then it became the stuff of legend! Just like the bent rim and the low hanging branch in our Playground that created both a challenge and an opportunity, these inner city Playground's had a magic all their own.

Could we do it again like that today?

CHAPTER THIRTY SIX: THE DAY PRESIDENT JOHN F KENNEDY WAS SHOT

Tenth grade: Cardinal O'Hara High School, Father Ryan's Religion Class.

The day President Kennedy was shot and killed, school was dismissed early. It's one of those seminal events in your life that stays with you forever. We went home, changed out of our school clothes, and by a power indescribable were drawn back to the Playground. Even though we were fifteen, and had moved on from the Playground to high school Sports and other after-school activities, on this day there was only one place we wanted to be: together at the Playground. We were confused and scared and the Playground provided the stability and reassurance we needed, as the world seem to be falling apart in Dallas on that horrible day.

We were also concerned for the younger guys still in the Playground who were even more afraid and confused than we were. We needed to be with them and tell them that we would all get through this .... together. We had to assure them that the world would somehow survive, even if we didn't totally believe it ourselves. This reassurance was teaching and mentoring at its most basic level, a skill that seems virtually lost in business today.

How many successful men 'give back' to their neighborhoods, trying to help those still striving to reach and achieve their goals? Most of our country's neighborhoods, schools, and civic associations, would benefit greatly from the experience and leadership that they could provide. Ironically, it would be these accomplished men who would benefit the most from giving their time. The words 'it is much better to give than to receive' are not shallow or misspoken, they're true!. These successful men, and the boys they helped, would be much better for having done it!

We returned to the Playground that day because it was a world where we had the control. In that atmosphere of 'free-play,' a diverse group of developing boys got to set the stage, make the rules, and learn to live with the outcome. Wouldn't it be a great thing if our most accomplished leader's would go back and reassure those that were still struggling in their old neighborhood's and towns? They would then stand as 'living examples' of what's possible, putting to rest the doubts of those who weren't sure if they could do it too. Ted Dean and Emlen Tunnell used to come back and visit our Playground when they were in town. We hung on their every word and those days were monumental in the annals of our Playground's history.

Although only a few year's older than the guys still there, we tried in our own way to give back and do what Emlen and Ted had done for us. On that fateful day, the Playground was our oasis in what seemed like a never ending desert of tragedy. As a group we learned that fear and difficulty are not nearly as daunting when we face them together. This is how war's are successfully fought and won, and how familie's and companie's band together to get through the hard times. Sticking together was how we got through that national day of mourning.

The Playground was there to provide the glue!

Dormant reminders of a gloried past

CHAPTER THIRTY SEVEN: SANDLOT AND MONKEY-BAR MEMORIES:

I can make it, I know I can make it. SPLASH! Hey, let me try again.

Like fine wine, and money invested well, our Playground experiences age and ripen, paying dividends our entire lives. The memories have become sweeter, the highs are much higher, and the lessons are now permanent. What we learned in the Playground was not forced on us, or a required field of study. It was rather a joyous celebration of what it meant to be young, growing better with every day in a world surrounded by wonder.

The first time I admitted that I liked a girl I was hanging upside down from the monkey-bars with two other guys. Just playing on the monkey-bars was breaking a major Playground rule. We figured if anyone caught us doing this we could just drop on our heads and end it all right there. Strangely enough, one of the other two guys not only liked girls, but liked the same one that I did too. These girls were known to hang around the monkey-bar and swing-set areas, and that's why we were there. It was separate from the rest of the Playground and they never came in any further than that. We just hoped and prayed that none of the other guys would see us. It was a risk that on that day seemed worth taking.

Trading one problem for another was just Playground barter and it happened all the time. One day you would rip your good school pants sliding into third base to beat the throw. You should have changed into your play clothes before coming to the Playground, but you didn't. It was going to get you in serious trouble when you got home, but man that was a great slide and it really made that third baseman mad. The beating you'd get from your Mom when you walked in the back door seemed like a good trade for the glory of that slide. A slide you'd probably never have made if you'd have taken the extra minutes necessary to change clothes. The thrashing your Mother gave you is now long forgotten, but the glory of that slide ....! It's as real in your memory today as when it happened back then.

Later in life, that slide into third would be replaced with a gamble on a late product introduction that saved the company, but the feeling was just the same. You risked it all and went for it. Based on all you had learned and with every instinct inside you it seemed like the right thing to do. You knew deep in your soul it was worth the gamble. You learned that and more in the hundreds of lessons taught inside the Playground's gate.

Who teaches those lessons today?

The lesson's of the sandlot are inside many of the board members running America's most successful companies today, but who is coming along to replace them? Those lessons are only different today in their time frame. The process of successful decision-making is still the same.

Choosing whether to risk that slide into third base, or gamble on the late product introduction all comes from the confidence and basic skills the Playground gave birth to. To finally admit that you liked girls was possible only because you felt your Playground reputation was well established and secure and hopefully beyond risk, but there was no guarantee. We learned that to get what you really wanted out of life, it sometimes meant 'laying it all on the line.' Win or lose, we never looked back. We picked up the pieces resulting from our decisions and moved on. That was the Playground's way and it set the course for all risk/reward opportunities as we moved on in life.

The players may grow older and change, but the game is still the same!

Every day we marveled at where this might lead

CHAPTER THIRTY EIGHT: THE BRIDGE OF POSSIBILITIES!

The Old Barn was across the creek. It was in the same run-down condition as the Bridge.

We had a decaying and crumbling bridge at the back of our park, only we didn't see it that way. The bridge used to cross the creek connecting the two sides of the estate that became our Playground. Now the middle span of the bridge had collapsed and was gone.

To us, the bridge represented all that was possible and still to be done. With pride, many of us wore scars from trying to cross the empty span of bridge that was no longer there. First we rigged up a tire swing. Then, when the tire wore out, we hung on for dear life to the rope, as we swung from one side to the other. Some of the more adventurous and daredevil among us, constructed a ramp, and tried to launch our bikes across the span, always falling short of the mark. Undeterred, we continued to find ways across that bridge, until one day in a big storm a large birch tree came down across the creek, just a short distance downstream from the bridge..

With teamwork and adolescent engineering, fifteen of us rolled that tree twenty feet upstream to the bridge. It was just long enough to connect both broken ends. We now had a permanent footpath across the creek. It was a Playground rite of passage the first time a new and younger boy got to 'walk the plank.' You were never quite the same once you successfully crossed the creek on that fallen tree. Instead of symbolizing something broken and destroyed, that bridge represented the challenge of all that was possible. Its spirit was still intact, even if a few parts of it were missing and that's where we came in.

We had continued to try and cross that bridge with every scheme our young imaginations could dream up. The bridge pointed the way and we did the rest. The direction was clear, even if there were a few obstacles to overcome. We jumped, swung, ramped, and catapulted across, always believing that we would make it. Then one day opportunity struck; that birch tree came down.

To us, this was a message from above. We now had permanent and easy access to both sides of our park. This all results from seeing into and through something that looked broken and destroyed. The bridge was still there, it just needed a little help from us to renew its purpose. It was great fun on the Fourth of July to see all the Dads, and many of the Moms, show off their dexterity as they also tried to 'walk the plank.'

In our current disposable and throwaway society, how many viable and valuable assets do we look away from and dismiss because the cosmetics need work? Maybe they even need major restoration. Many of these 'sleeping' assets are the answers to the questions we don't even ask. If we look into our corporate histories, many of the successful business strategies and projects from the past need only to be dusted off and updated to be brought back to life. The foundations, principles and structure are still there, waiting for us to realize the treasure buried right beneath our nose. Like the bridge with the missing part in the Playground, these successful but dormant corporate assets need only one important catalyst to come back to life and become readapted to success in the present.

That catalyst is us!

Just like that broken bridge, a stalled sales plan, a flawed marketing philosophy, or low company morale can all be fixed by having everyone look across that span together. Doing that can get **your corporate tree** across the creek. The process will build teamwork, create a renewed company vision, and bring out strengths in the workforce that no one previously knew were there.

Who really knows where that rebuilt bridge is likely to lead!

CHAPTER THIRTY NINE: WE DON'T DREAM NEARLY ENOUGH

Connie Mack Stadium: Bottom of the ninth and Behm's up to bat .... "Kurt, wake up, you're late for school"

Most good things that happen in life start with a dream. In America, we used to be a country of dreamers. American dreamers split the atom, built Hoover Dam and the Empire State Building, and one dreamer dropped out of school, to develop software so we could all be computer whizzes.

Today, we don't dream nearly enough.

One of the best parts of a good day at the Playground was coming home and telling your exploits to your Mom and Dad. Later, after going to bed, you would lie there, replaying over and over in your mind again what you had done. You would dream about how that next homerun was going to be even longer, or how that hook shot would sink from forty, not twenty feet away. The dreams you carried inside you had a wonderful quality, and many of them did in fact come true. You did eventually sink that forty-foot hook shot, and hit that homerun over the fence in deep center field into Mrs. Burrough's back yard, but it all started with a dream.

The Playground was a place of dreams, our dreams, and we dreamed them together! We didn't know the meaning of the word vicarious, but we all lived out each other's dreams too. After all, that other guy was from our Playground and that meant that a little bit of his exploits had to rub off on us, and ours on him! Dreams to us were an affirmation of what was possible. In many cultures, dreams and dreaming are the foundations and bedrock of what they believe. In Native American Society, dreams and visions are what one searches for, some for their entire lifetime. Tibetan and Eastern Indian culture share variations of this dream state also.

If you talk to almost anyone who has achieved greatness, they always seem to enjoy talking more about when their concept was only a dream than when it became the finished product. Dreams are about not having barriers and the endless possibilities that lie within the human spirit, and the will to achieve. This is exactly what the Playground represented to us and it had the systems in place to show you how to turn your dreams into reality. If you've lost the ability to dream and see past your immediate self, then maybe you should go back and revisit your Playground. If it's now physically gone, it should still exist somewhere in the recesses of your memory.

I hope and pray that in some way, it's still there.

CHAPTER FORTY: TAKE AWAYS

Been there, done that, you say! I'll believe you, if you
grew up in a Playground.

What happened inside the Playground is not nearly as important as what we took away from it. I'm walking with my dog tonight and thinking about how the Playground and its lessons have affected every part of my life, and in so many ways shaped it. Even now, the Playground is a living thing inside me, but more than that, it actually is me. Aren't all the best things in life that way? We experience them first outside of ourselves, then we internalize them and they become a big part of who we are.

Many chapter's in our lives have a beginning and an end, but the Playground endures. It has achieved immortality inside the Men that played there. We carry with us in our hearts and imagination's, the feelings and friendships we made there which can never die. The Playground gave order to my life then, and it gives order and special meaning to my life now. When doubt and confusion surface in my life, I travel back in my memory to the Playground. There, I could always find an answer to my problems, no matter how serious or profound. A wise coach once said to me "when it starts to get really confusing, go back to blocking and tackling." Basic stuff! The Playground sent the same message.

Those were, and are, answers for a lifetime.

No matter what kind of day you had in school, or what might have happened at home, the Playground was always there. It was a spiritual oasis in a world where the answers were not always clear. It was there that you could 'plug back in' to who you were, and maybe

151

more important, to who you would someday be. The Playground was all about potential and it existed on many different levels. I know I've used the word 'Playground' a lot, but it really was a developmental panacea. It was a place where boys could turn into men and live out their dreams. The combination of their rapid adolescent growth, turned loose in an atmosphere of 'free play,' created the magic.

In time, this magic created, a Man!

I'm not saying there are no other ways or places to learn to become a man. The Playground just did it consistently, did it right, and made it fun while it was happening. You got to see your dreams realized as an eight year old in what the older boys had already accomplished, and you were given a ladder to climb to realize those dreams for yourself.

I've seen nothing else doing that today!

CHAPTER FORTY ONE: ANYWHERE USA- THE PLAYGROUND AS A STATE OF MIND

"Show me your friends and I'll tell you who you are."
Sister Marcella: 8th Grade, St. Thomas of Villanova
Grade School, circa 1962.

Since the Playground was primarily a state of mind, its nature was transplantable and portable to wherever kids could play freely. Every day was a day of wonder in the Playground. You could never be sure of what would happen or to whom, but you knew it would be unlike the day before, and also the day after. The stories you told about it would often be better than the actual events themselves.

The Homeruns were always hit OVER Mrs. Burrough's roof, and the touchdown passes were always at least eighty yards long, even though none of us could throw the ball even thirty yards. The dunks always seemed to happen only when there was no one else around to see them. The stories were bigger than the actual events because we needed them to be that way. That was what our imaginations saw. That was the scope and the vision the Playground gave birth to.

Heroic deeds were commonplace in the Playground, but never common. The rules had to be obeyed, but envelopes were pushed. That's how you became a Playground legend. No one had to tell you about risk taking, that came naturally. You knew there was a safety net of older and more experienced guys, always there to cushion your fall and to counsel you on how to get back up again.

Getting back up was one of the most important lessons
the Playground taught.

After all it was OK to fail, but you always had to get back up after giving it your best try. Never quitting was one of the most fundamental 'Commandments of the Playground.' As I mentioned before, cowboys like to use the phrase "that guy has a lot of try in him." In the Playground, you couldn't truly belong if you didn't at least try. No silent observers here, everyone's limits were tested and everyone's comfort zone was stretched. The message was, if you try your best, it's OK to occasionally fail, but it's still much better to win!

As cowboys also know, a sense of humor helped a lot too!

The kid who grew up playing stickball in the Bronx, and whose parents then moved to San Antonio would quickly adapt to the new games on the Texas Playground. Although the rules might be different, the sense of the game, and the feelings you got playing it were much the same. Those feelings of togetherness, that forged your emerging identity, were all fostered by 'free-play.' They created lifelong bonds and memories within the boys that played together. Those feelings developed into the catalysts within a mans character that he could count on. They were benchmarks of his growth that helped him make the right decisions as he moved on with life. Just as the flavor and retelling of our Playground stories grew and expanded over time, the motivational effect of the Playground experience became stronger too.

That state of mind may be waning today, but it's still there. It's there in the hearts and minds of the millions of middle aged men that *'made their bones'* on the Playgrounds of America. We need to reinvent the possibility of 'free-play' for our children, so that they can reinvigorate our families, our neighborhoods, our corporations, and ultimately our nation. Our greatest leaders such as Abraham Lincoln, Teddy Roosevelt, and Ronald Reagan never lost the magic within themselves that was first developed by the magic of 'free-play.'

And neither should we!

Waiting for their Lifeblood (The Kids) to return

CHAPTER FORTY TWO: THEY STAND GUARD

I pressed the button, but the darn thing didn't come on.
How are we going to get that lock open on the gate now
without a flashlight? I told you to change the batteries
....

Many of the Playgrounds of our youth are still there, but standing idle most of the time. They are used only for parent supervised activities like Little League, T-Ball, Soccer Practice, and Day Camp. The freewheeling, multi-age, four season, kid run, mecca's of 'free-play' sadly are now gone. These still standing empty parks have become testaments to our pasts, arteries drained of all blood, sans the Fourth of July Baby Parade, or a place for the annual Antique Car Show. The blood was provided by the kids who used to play there. Now they are like power sources with their plugs pulled out,

They have become the old age homes for trees, with initials carved high up on their trunks, marking significant dates and immortalizing historic Playground events of the past. If you listen hard, you can still hear the laughter, the screams of triumph, and the octave higher voices of the boys who went on to become the men of my generation. To see and hear these things you have to recognize the signs. What you can see only with your eyes, and hear only with your ears is hollow. It's what you hear and remember inside your heart that makes the difference. You had to grow up in some form of Playground, engaged in the ecstasy of 'free-play,' to now feel the loss that comes when passing an abandoned Playground. They sit devoid of their purpose, in an age that has lost not only its innocence, but also its direction.

Like developmental antiques, these Playgrounds are truly appreciated only by those who left something of themselves there. We needed the Playground then, and it was always there for us. Now the Playground calls out to us in its abandonment and despair, having become nothing more than a vacant distant image of the once 'maker of men.' It worked because we were together in unrestricted play, 'free-play,' and being together created the magic. That magic has now gone. Father to Son, Teacher to Student, Employer to Employee, they all need the one thing so missing in our lives today; a real connection. To be connected, something has to be shared. It could be a value system, a game plan, or a simple goal to be performed together, but something has to be shared and there has to be time set aside to share it!

The Playground never ran out of time for us to be together as a group.

It's hard to do that when the 'I' mentality seems to pervade all aspects of our modern lives. The Playground would not have understood the 'me' generation, nor called them its own. The 'I' mentality is not limited to the tennis or golf course, or the music and movies that pretend to entertain. It enters the corporate boardroom too. Grandstanding, and poor self-serving judgment, many times replace what used to be an overall concern for the good of the company.

Numerous stories have surfaced recently about high-ranking executives manipulating stock prices, raiding corporate pension and profit sharing plans, and providing false and misleading information to suit their own personal gains.

Greed is good only if you're greedy! The Playground and most of the Men it produced were above that.

I read an article recently by a four star Army General. He was expressing doubts about our country's ability to fight a major war because we no longer share a common value system. How can we? We applaud and celebrate only our differences, instead of uniting and bonding around our common strengths and beliefs. Just look at our political system today; it has polarized our society with 'divide and conquer' as its battle cry, Corporate America following right behind.

The abandoned Playgrounds, both in our neighborhoods and our minds, cry out for us to look back and remember. We can't allow the current era of drugs, violence, and misguided media, to control our children, children that are now manufactured, rather than raised. We can't let science and technology totally steal our innocence, one that brought out the best in who we were, and then could possibly be.

I ask you now to look back. Look back and remember a time when you really belonged to something. Remember when it all mattered and you didn't feel so alone. If we don't, we'll continue to deny where we are and what we've lost, trumping any answer that doesn't suit our immediate gratification and the hole in our hearts will still be there. A hole that we can deny with our reason and intellect, but not in what we feel. A hole that is bigger and deeper than any of the arguments to deny it. If we ignore our history and are doomed to repeat it, then in what form of rebirth can the Playground emerge?

And what lessons if any, will it then have to tell?

CLOSING THOUGHTS

I started to write 'Final Thoughts' as this chapter's title. Then I realized that these will not be my final thoughts about the Playground and the profound effects it has had on my life. I hope it will not be your last thoughts about it either. If the things discussed seem simplistic and out of date, I ask you to take a closer look. The problems we deal with today are not anecdotal, but fundamental. We often treat only the symptoms while the malady spreads. If the problems seem unfixable to you, then I suggest you may be trying to fix them without the proper tools at your disposal. Those tools that the Playground provided.

I wrote this book because we often forget that sometimes you have to reach backwards so that you can then move ahead. We push so hard today into the future; with new technologies, systems, projections and forecasts, that we are oftentimes lulled into leaving the best parts of ourselves behind. I don't believe we are ever going to find the world that we want, or be able to live in it happily, unless we bring to that world the very best part of ourselves.

It was the very best part of all of us that was soaring around third base, trying to beat that throw from the outfield. We were not worrying or focusing on being tagged out at home (the negative), but dreaming of the glory of scoring the winning run, and being carried off the field by the guys. That same spirit would also convince us that flipping a Mantle card for a Mazeroski card was a good move because today you couldn't lose. If you did you'd be heartsick, but you knew you could live with it.

The prospect of losing never dampened our desire, or the attempt to win.

Yes, there were always losers, but that was temporary. Later today, tomorrow or Friday, they would be winners too. It was the feeling that came along with winning that made everything worthwhile. Not one boy ever came out of the Playground after his eight-year tenure, worse than when he went in. From eight to eleven we admired and imitated the older guys and their exploits were implanted into our dreams. From twelve to fourteen we were then able to live them out for ourselves. Mark Twain knew this acutely and brought it to life in his epic novel 'Tom Sawyer.' It's a classic book about two boys on a series of misadventures and explorations that would create lessons inside of them that would last a lifetime. The book endures because the process of male adolescent development is as old as the great Mississippi River itself, and the surrounding valleys that formed their Playground.

Nor was I writing in the spirit of the popular movie 'Field of Dreams,' with the message of 'build it, and they will come.' I wrote because the Playground's are still there, it's we who are now gone. For those of us lucky enough to have passed through its gates, the message it gave forever will be coursing through our souls. The Playground took on our persona as much as we did its. It was in every way a living, breathing thing that we carried inside us.

And the best eight years of our life!

If there is an answer to filling the void in our society created by the death of our Playgrounds and their lifeblood 'free-play,' it's going to take more than money. It will take a passionate commitment by the very institutions that stand to gain the most; America's businesses and corporations! If every company in America adopted one local Playground in their own town or city, and staffed it with a full-time custodian, then maybe, just maybe, we could recreate some of the magic. These custodians would be screened and then trained in the concept of 'free-play.' The ones that I would suggest for the jobs already know and understand it from their own past experience.

They would ideally be Senior Citizens, with the hands-on experience and understanding of having raised their own children in the Playground era, coupled with having gone through it themselves. They would provide a safety net for the superstructure of the Playground without intruding on the games, rules, culture, and adventures created

162

by the kids who play there. They would be an arms-length insurance policy against unsavory elements entering the Playground, and a cell phone contact for parents needing to check and confirm that their children are safe.

What better public relations could a company have with its local community than to be an active participant in the positive development of that communities youth? We actually had one of these custodians in my Playground, but he was only there about two hours a day because he had three other Playgrounds under his care. He put out the bases on the ball-field in the morning and he took them back in at night. He cut the Playground's grass and locked the main gate after it got dark. He also had one eye on everything that was going on inside the fence while he was there, but you would never have known it. He never intruded on any of the games or the political structures that enforced them.

With a very minimal investment from companies with vision, we could possibly start a new system of individual development in an atmosphere driven by the powerful magic only 'free-play' can provide. I believe we, as a society would benefit greatly from the result! It would also be great for the many 'seniors,' who don't want to be totally idle in their retirements. It would give them a great opportunity to share what they've learned with a new generation of boys in desperate need of their lessons. It could have a greater impact on our society as a whole than any other one thing we could do.

To my way of thinking, a win-win!

MACRONE PARK

My Playground was at the corner of Conestoga and Rockingham Roads, in a suburb of Philadelphia called Rosemont. Our particular corner of Rosemont was Garrett Hill.

Garrett Hill had a very mixed and diverse group of residents, even more so by 1950's standards.

We had almost every race and nationality represented in our little neighborhood. Several famous people had come from Garrett Hill and the neighborhoods nearby, such as Anna Moffo the Opera Singer, Mary Casatt the painter, and of course Ted Dean and Emlen Tunnell both of N.F.L. fame.

This book however is really not their story.

This is the story of all those 'regular' boys that played and developed into men on my Playground and on the thousands of Playgrounds all over America. It's the story of how they came up through the Playground system, a system geographically diverse, while at its heart similar regardless of location. It existed in some form and in all sections of our country until the late 1960's.

It is in the hopes of preserving some part of that system, if only in our hearts and memory, that

I began to write ....

TO REMEMBER:

If you can remember a time when your mind saw only the good, always looking away from the bad, there is probably a Playground still protecting those memories .... even today!

MY WISH FOR YOU:

In the hopes that one Playground will be forever saved, the one you carry inside.

Breinigsville, PA USA
17 September 2009
224251BV00001B/60/P

9 781438 937144